Forecasting
Methods

Forecasting Methods

ROGER K. CHISHOLM
Associate Professor of Economics
College of Business Administration
Memphis State University

and

GILBERT R. WHITAKER, JR.
Dean: M. J. Neeley School of Business
Texas Christian University

1971

RICHARD D. IRWIN, INC., Homewood, Illinois 60430

Irwin-Dorsey Limited, Georgetown, Ontario   L7G 4B3

FIRST PRINTING, MAY, 1971
SECOND PRINTING, MARCH, 1972
THIRD PRINTING, AUGUST, 1972
FOURTH PRINTING, JANUARY, 1973
FIFTH PRINTING, JANUARY, 1974
SIXTH PRINTING, OCTOBER, 1974
SEVENTH PRINTING, DECEMBER, 1974
EIGHTH PRINTING, JUNE, 1975
NINTH PRINTING, AUGUST, 1975
TENTH PRINTING, NOVEMBER, 1975
ELEVENTH PRINTING, AUGUST, 1976
TWELFTH PRINTING, MARCH, 1977

Library of Congress Catalog Card No. 75-153165

PRINTED IN THE UNITED STATES OF AMERICA

To   Jean
Ruth

Preface

This book began when Professor Whitaker was assigned to teach a course in business forecasting at Northwestern University. A quick survey of existing material failed to turn up a text which covered the topics which he believed should be covered. Over time, a file of materials was collected and a set of lecture notes took shape. When Whitaker left Northwestern for Washington University, Professor Chisholm continued the course, modifying the content to suit his interests and skills. This collaboration in the preparation of the materials for this book has hopefully produced a whole which is more than the sum of the parts.

This book provides background material and references which are useful in teaching a course in business forecasting. Much of the learning in such a course comes from practice. Thus, we believe that students (or practitioners) should tackle significant forecasting projects as a major part of their educational efforts. Such projects should require "hands-on" experience in the science and art of forecasting. This book could also serve as desk-top reference material for use in a number of business and economics courses where forecasts are required.

Many people have been helpful in the preparation of this material for publication. Students at Northwestern have read drafts in the critical manner that only students can. Mrs. Ann Crost at Northwestern University and Mrs. Ruth Scheetz at Washington University have typed many drafts competently. Also at Washington University, Mrs. Jane Warren provided critical and helpful editorial assistance.

April, 1971   ROGER K. CHISHOLM

GILBERT R. WHITAKER, JR.

Contents

——8—— Additional Regression Problems and Techniques

——9—— Forecasting: Art and Science

Index

chapter
—1—
Introduction

IMPORTANCE AND NECESSITY OF FORECASTS

Forecasts are required in all situations in which a current choice or decision has future implications. For example, a man who decides to take his fourth drink is forecasting that it will or will not have certain aftereffects. More to the point, a board of directors which agrees to spend $10 million on plant expansion is forecasting or accepting staff-prepared forecasts that the demand for the firm's products will profitably utilize the new capacity. Routine reorders of stock for a supply room or a retail store also rest on either explicit or implied forecasts of future needs or sales.

Good decision making can become better or worse, depending on the quality of the forecasts which underlie the decision-making process. Many decisions are relatively routine, relate only to the very near future, and/or involve relatively small gains or losses. For such decisions, simple assumptions that the future will be much like the past are adequate forecasts.

Gains from using sophisticated forecasting techniques would not cover the cost.

However, many short-run decisions accumulate into a long-run course of action, and many decisions commit large amounts of money for long periods of time. When the monetary gains or losses may be large, the gains in terms of an improved decision from a formal forecast will by and large offset the cost of the forecast.

This book was written for those who desire knowledge of formal techniques for making better forecasts. In some cases, formal techniques cannot improve on informed judgment. However, knowledge of the value of formal forecasting methods can only come through a test of the efficacy of formal methods. Forecasting the future remains in large measure an art. Like any artist, a good forecaster must be a skilled technician in whose hands the work of art evolves. Scientific tools should help a good forecasting artist to become a great one.

WHO USES FORECASTS?

Although in the past the major user of forecasts has been business, many other users can be identified. Governments, from local school districts up to the federal government, prepare and use a wide variety of forecasts. Nonprofit organizations such as welfare agencies, foundations, universities, and hospitals prepare and use forecasts. The forecasting models described in this text could be used equally well by forecasters for any organization. However, most of the examples are business applications, and our discussion concerns their use within the business organization.

In accordance with the traditional functional classification of business activities, forecasts are needed for marketing, production, and financial planning. Further, top management needs forecasts for planning and implementing long-term objectives. The amount of detail and frequency of need for forecasts varies among specific users within firms and among different types of industries, depending on markets and technology. Thus the uses can only be described quite generally.

Marketing uses of forecasts are perhaps the most obvious. The planning of sales strategies depends in great measure on demand expectations. It may be that the marketing manager's reaction to a specific forecast is to plan marketing actions whose desired effect is to make the forecast incorrect; thus a revised forecast will become necessary after the formulation of marketing plans. Forecasts may be required by total market, by regions, by months, by weeks, etc. The methods to be discussed in this book can be applied in most of these categories, provided that adequate data are collected for the analysis.

Production planners need the most detailed forecasts in order to schedule production activities, order raw materials, hire workers, and plan shipments. When it comes to actual production, the forecasts must be in terms of exactly what colors and styles will be required for shipment at what times. Normally the lead times of production forecasts are quite short, and moderate errors are absorbed in inventory fluctuations.

Financial managers use sales forecasts to plan their cash and borrowing positions during the year. Great detail by product lines is not necessary, but the cash implications of product forecasts are required. Long-term forecasts are necessary for the planning of changes in a firm's capital structure. Decisions to issue stock or undertake debt in order to maintain the desired financial structure of the firm require forecasts of money-market conditions.

Top management requires forecasts for planning capital expenditures for new plant and equipment, for planning major promotional activities, and for planning the general direction and future course for the firm. All of these activities are critical for the success and survival of the business.

FORECAST ACCURACY

The accuracy necessary depends on the use to which the forecasts are to be put and the ease with which the firm can react to unexpected events. Accuracy can be measured in a variety of ways. For example, accuracy could be measured in terms of percentage deviations from the level of the variable

FIGURE 1–1

Forecast versus Actual Changes

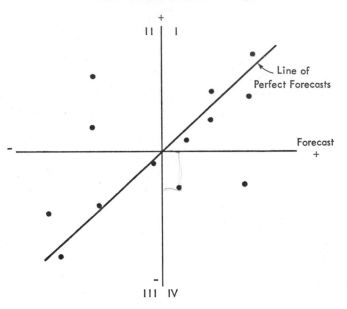

being forecast. Nevertheless, it may be more important to know the direction of change than the absolute level, in which case accuracy would be measured in terms of the numbers of turning points forecast accurately.

A useful graphical way of showing a forecast's ability to predict actual events is to use a four-quadrant graph on which forecast changes are plotted against the actual changes. Figure 1–1 shows such a graph. Actual changes are measured along the vertical axis, and forecast changes are measured along the horizontal axis. The diagonal line represents perfect forecasts. All points in the second and fourth quadrants represent forecasts which missed the actual direction of change. This type of graphic scheme lends itself to analytical uses as well. The topic of forecast accuracy and evaluation will be considered more fully in a later chapter.[1]

LINKING MACRO AND MICRO FORECASTS

Several levels of aggregation in forecasts can be distinguished. That is, forecasts may be made for individual items or for combinations of items, up to and including the entire national output for some time period. The national economy is usually the highest level of aggregation in which business forecasters have interest. However, some highly aggregated subset of GNP may be of prime interest to a business forecaster. For instance a forecaster for a firm in the heavy construction industry may be more interested in a forecast of business plant and equipment expenditures than of the total gross national product or disposable personal income.

Industry sales forecasts are of considerable importance to planners or forecasters in the large firms in the U.S. economy. Firm sales forecasts are often based on previously determined industry forecasts. Industry forecasts are usually made conditional on forecasts of the economy as a whole or of a major subsector.

There is an apparent hierarchy of forecasts: first, the national economy, then major subsectors, by the industry as a whole, and then sales by a particular firm. Inside the firm there is also a hierarchy of forecasts: from total dollar sales of the firm, to dollar and unit sales by product line, down to

---

[1] For a study evaluating forecast accuracy, see Victor Zarnowitz, *An Appraisal of Short-Term Economic Forecasts,* Occasional Paper 104 (New York: National Bureau of Economic Research, 1967).

periodic sales by model. Each type of forecast is utilized at each level of the hierarchy.

PLAN OF THE BOOK

This book deals largely with techniques of forecasting. The primary concern is with quantitative techniques which can be used to produce forecasts. Most of the methods described can readily be programmed for computer computation. Indeed, programs are available for most of the procedures discussed.

Not all forecasting techniques are included since many of the simulation techniques dear to the heart of the marketing man are beyond the scope of this text. The market survey, as such, is also excluded.

Some simple examples of applications of the various techniques are included. In some cases the example is nothing more than a vehicle for the discussion of the technique though, as has been pointed out above, applications in government and other organizations also exist. The reader is required to furnish some amount of imagination and ingenuity in order to determine how any given technique fits his situation.

Chapter 2 discusses so-called "naïve" methods, forecasts which are based solely on manipulation of the data series to be forecast. Several of these methods are described.

Opinion polls and survey techniques are the subject of Chapter 3. Sometimes called "loaded deck" methods, they assume that one can obtain accurate forecasts by asking people their intentions.

In Chapter 4 the use of barometric or indicator forecasts is discussed. Since the use of indicators, particularly in conjunction with other methods, is widespread a forecaster should be aware of their advantages and limitations.

Opportunistic forecasting and, in particular, the opportunistic GNP forecasting method of John Lewis are described in

Chapter 5. "Opportunistic" as used here means a variety of methods used to produce a forecast.

Input-output analysis has wide promise as a method of producing sector-industry forecasts consistent with particular GNP forecasts. Its use in forecasting is discussed in Chapter 6.

Chapters 7 and 8 are concerned with model building and the estimation of the parameters of the models by means of regression analysis. The presence of two chapters on regression should not deceive the reader into placing too much emphasis on this one tool of the forecaster. Nevertheless, this powerful technique is a complex and by no means elementary subject requiring considerable discussion. While the formal proofs of an econometrics text are absent, regression analysis is developed heuristically in a forecasting context. In Chapter 7 the discussion is carried through single-equation, multiple linear regression. More advanced topics are developed in Chapter 8, where the discussion terminates with the use of multiequation, simultaneous-system, macro models.

Chapter 9 is of the nature of a post log. Such topics as the role of the forecaster, choice of forecasting models, and evaluation of forecasts are developed.

chapter
—2—
Naïve Forecasting Methods

The term *naïve* may be applied to any forecast obtained solely from historical values of the variables to be forecast. The forecast is prepared from previous observations of the forecast variable with no attempt to examine or recognize interrelationships with other variables. If the problem is to forecast sales of a product, only past levels of sales of the product are used to prepare the forecast.

Naïve should not be confused with *simple*. The techniques for manipulation of data may be very complex, as will be seen in the discussion of time-series analysis. The value of naïve forecasts is that they may be prepared relatively inexpensively and quickly. A naïve forecast may be implicit if no formal forecast is prepared. The businessman simply proceeds as if the future will resemble the recent past. Thus, his behavior implies a naïve forecast that the next period will be the same as the present or last period. The tendency to dismiss naïve forecasts because of their ease of preparation must be resisted. In many instances the naïve forecast serves as a standard of comparison. Complex forecasting techniques, which tend to be costly should be rejected unless they are an improvement upon naïve forecasts.

NAÏVE MODELS

Naïve models may be divided into two classes, though the dividing line between the groups is not always well defined. One group would consist of simple projection models. These models require inputs of data from recent observations, but no formal statistical analysis is performed. This does not mean that such forecasts could not be prepared on a computer. Because of their simplicity, such models, programmed for computer solution, could well be used to prepare large numbers of forecasts on a frequent basis, perhaps hour by hour.

The second group consists of models which, while naïve, are complex enough to warrant computer solution. Traditional time-series analysis, link-relative models, and exponential smoothing models are some examples.

1. Simple Naïve Models

Simple Projection Techniques. The simplest naïve models assume that recent past periods are the best predictors of the immediate future. Most models of this type do not give any explicit guidance as to which past periods are relevant, how many to consider, or what importance to attach to the various periods.

The simplest model would be

$$\hat{X}_{t+1} = X_t \qquad (2\text{--}1)$$

where X stands for the variable to be forecast, the subscripts refer to the period of time involved, and the $\wedge$ identifies a forecast value as distinguished from an observed datum. Thus, if X stands for product sales in either revenue or unit terms, this model forecasts sales for the next day or week to be the same as the present day or week.

For example, the last entry in Table 2–1 is 266. Using the above described forecasting model, this observation (266) would become the forecast for January of Year 7.

TABLE 2–1

Monthly Sales of Metal Containers
(units)

Month	Years					
	1	2	3	4	5	6
January..........	228	224	258	261	283	305
February.........	213	240	251	275	259	298
March...........	238	272	281	317	294	367
April............	272	306	307	484	521	291
May.............	268	303	373	305	312	334
June............	323	385	385	390	350	406
July.............	411	406	431	428	457-5	475 7
August..........	461	510	528	568	531-4	551 8
September........	446	442	452	504	483	528 –
October..........	348	336	499	497	374	427
November........	306	260	212	226	266	296
December........	111	275	249	228	261	266
Total.......	3625	3995	4226	4483	4395	4544

Although such methods are easy to use, there are problems which are readily apparent. The remedies which may be applied are in part suggested by the nature of the difficulties. For example, the data may not be very up-to-date, in which case, the forecaster's task may be to speed up the collection and reporting of the necessary data. Otherwise he will have to forecast the current value of the variable before he can prepare a forecast of the future. Another problem which the forecaster faces is the possibility that management may try to assure that the forecast is wrong; or management decisions may contribute to substantial variability in the data such that the observations are of little use to the forecaster. For example, a special sales-promotion effort during a particular month may distort results of the months before and after as well as of the month itself.

If a definite trend in the series being forecast exists, the above model will yield forecasts which are persistently too high or too low, depending on the direction of the trend. Here the obvious answer is to incorporate the trend into the projection model. One possibility of incorporating trends is given in (2–2).

$$\hat{X}_{t+1} = X_t + (X_t - X_{t-1}) \qquad (2\text{–}2)$$

This model adds the latest observed absolute period-to-period change to the most recent observed level of the variable. For some purposes, the rate of change may be of more interest than the absolute amount and may be incorporated as in (2–3).

$$\hat{X}_{t+1} = X_t\left(\frac{X_t}{X_{t-1}}\right) \qquad (2\text{–}3)$$

Equation (2–2), using information from Table 2–1, yields a forecast for January of Year 7 of

$$\hat{X}_{t+1} = 266 + (266 - 296) = 266 - 30 = 236.$$

Of course, visual inspection of the data reveals that the model is inappropriate, since no strong trend is evident. Let us ignore this defect in order to complete the illustration; the forecast computed from Equation (2–3) is

$$\hat{X}_{t+1} = 266\left(\frac{266}{296}\right) = 266(.8986) = 239$$

In each case the future change is assumed to be the same as the most recent absolute or percentage change. Only one period's change or rate of change has been used in the computations.

It is likely, however, that the forecaster would want to use an average of past absolute changes or rates of change in preparing his forecast. Models of this type may be represented by

$$\hat{X}_{t+1} = X_t + \frac{\sum_{i=0}^{n} [X_{t-i} - X_{t-(i+1)}]}{n+1} \qquad \text{absolute change} \quad (2\text{-}4)$$

$$\hat{X}_{t+1} = X_t \left[\sum_{i=0}^{n} \frac{X_{t-i}}{X_{t-(i+1)}} \right] \frac{1}{n+1} \qquad \text{rate of change} \quad (2\text{-}5)$$

where n is the number of changes averaged. The choice of n is arbitrary in both cases.

Let $n = 2$ and use the data from Table 2–1. The forecast from Equation (2–4) is

$$\hat{X}_{t+1} = 266 + \frac{(266 - 296) + (296 - 427) + (427 - 528)}{3}$$
$$= 266 + \frac{-30 - 131 - 107}{3}$$
$$= 266 - 89 = 177$$

and from Equation (2–5)

$$\hat{X}_{t+1} = 266 \frac{\left(\frac{266}{296} + \frac{296}{427} + \frac{427}{528}\right)}{3}$$
$$= 266 \left(\frac{.8696 + .6932 + .8087}{3}\right)$$
$$= 266 \left(\frac{2.3715}{3}\right) = 266(.7905) = 210$$

It is important to note that the choice of n may affect the result. A less arbitrary choice might have been to compute the average over the past year. For these data a different forecast would obtain. It is important to note that not all series are sensitive to the time period chosen. This is *especially true* when a strong trend is observed, in which case the above models would be appropriate and would forecast well. There is apparently some variation in the data which is more important than trends and is strongly influencing the forecasts.

Visual inspection of the data in Table 2–1 indicates that seasonal variation seems to exist. Seasonal variation can be described as fluctuations in the time series which occur with

FIGURE 2–1

Tier Chart for Monthly Sales of Metal Containers (years 1–3)

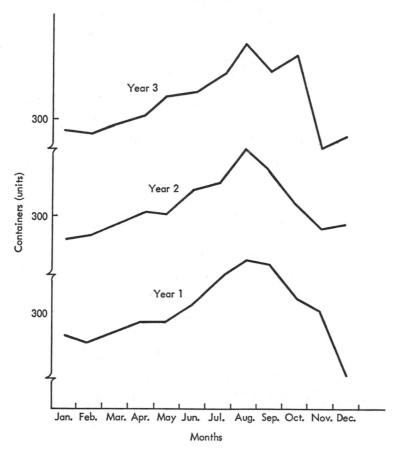

some consistency over the same time spans. The tier chart shown in Figure 2–1 illustrates this variation dramatically. There are naïve models which enable the forecaster to take advantage of such a periodic pattern of results.

If the variable being used in the forecast typically changes substantially from month to month and the months tend to be similar in successive years, then the model might be

$$\hat{X}_{t+1} = X_{t-11} \qquad (2\text{-}6)$$

Since t is the index of months, this equation says that next month the variable will take on the same value it did in the corresponding month one year ago. This equation, using the data in Table 2–1, yields a forecast of 305 for January of Year 7. For time series with a very strong seasonal pattern, the forecasting model might be generalized to

$$\hat{X}_{t+T} = X_{t+T-12} \qquad (2\text{-}7)$$

where T is the number of periods (months in this case) from the present to the period to be forecast. For example, if a forecast is to be prepared in July of Year 6, then $t = 7$. If the forecast is for September, then $T = 2$. Thus

$$\hat{X}_{7+2} = X_9 = X_{7+2-12} = X_{-3} \qquad (2\text{-}8)$$

where January (of Year 6) $= 1$; December (of Year t) $= 0$; November $= -1$; October $= -2$; September $= -3$ which is the desired result—i.e., the best forecast for any month is the same month the preceding year. The entry for September of Year 5 in Table 2–1 is 483. This is the forecast determined by (2–7) for September of Year 6. It may be seen that an underestimate resulted.

The major weakness of the above approach is that it ignores all information generated since the relevant month last year. If, in addition to a seasonal factor, there has also been growth or decline, the forecaster is not able to use such information in the above models. There are numerous ways of introducing more recent information. For example, one possible means of combining a seasonal and trend variation into a naïve model would be

Lousy model

$$\hat{X}_{t+1} = X_{t-11} \times 12 \left[1 - \left(\frac{X_t[X_{(t-13)}]}{X_{t-1}[X_{(t-12)}]} \right) \right] \qquad (2\text{–}9)$$

The term within the brackets is the seasonally adjusted monthly rate of growth over the past two corresponding *pairs* of months. This figure is multiplied by 12 to obtain the estimated yearly rate of growth. The result is in turn multiplied by the observed level of the variable for the relevant month a year ago to yield a forecast of the level of the variable for the next month. The forecast is

$$\hat{X}_{t+1} = 305 \left[12 \left(1 - \frac{266(266)}{296(261)} \right) \right]$$

$$= 305 \left[12 \left(1 - \frac{70756}{77256} \right) \right]$$

$$= 305[12(1 - .9159)] = 305[12(.0841)]$$

$$= 305(1.0092) = 307.8$$

From the above discussion, it should be apparent that not all the possibilities have been presented. The number and complexity of naive models which could be devised are limited only by the imagination and ingenuity of the forecaster.

The really skillful forecaster should also be able to devise systematic means of inserting into the forecasts his subjective feelings about how the variables might be expected to change.

2. More Complex Naïve Models

The following three models are also suggestive of several possibilities which the forecaster may employ. Each in turn has variations. Wide availability of computer programs for the solution of these models argues for their inclusion here. The techniques discussed are traditional time-series analysis, link-relative methods, and exponential smoothing.

Traditional Time-Series Analysis. Complete discussion of this topic is not attempted here, as the area of time-series analysis has reached such a state of development that entire books are devoted to it. The bibliography to this chapter lists several detailed sources. The present discussion concentrates on the concepts of time-series analysis. The how-to-do-it discussion must be in terms of the specific computation machinery and programs *available* to the forecaster. Most follow the general pattern of one of almost a dozen versions of Census Method II or the Bureau of Labor Statistics Seasonal Factor Method. The procedural details depend on which of these is available to the forecaster, but the underlying assumptions are basically the same.

Decomposition of the raw data of a time series into components, each of which may be analyzed separately, is central to classical time-series analysis. A number of possible decompositions exist. However, only the model and the related procedures of the above-mentioned programs will be discussed here.

A time series is nothing more than a series of statistical observations made over a period of time. Presumably the rules of collection and method of computation remain the same, while the magnitude of the phenomenon being measured varies. Typically, successive elements of the time series are of similar magnitude, and differences in magnitude are more likely between widely separated elements. This is reasonable, because the underlying forces which caused the series to take on a particular value in one time period tend to change but little in the next time period. Further, for some series there may be a direct causal influence of the magnitude of the variable in one period on the magnitude of that variable in the next.

Time-series analysis, being a naïve technique, depends upon manipulation of the observed series. The assumption is that there are regular and repeating components which interact to produce the total series. The task is to identify each of these components. Knowing something about each of the parts, the forecaster may then say something about the expected value of the series in some future period. The models discussed here assume that there are four components which will completely decompose any time series. The four components are seasonal variation, secular trend, cyclical variation, and irregular fluctuations. It goes without saying that, if the forecaster feels that his particular time series does not fit these models, other procedures should be sought.

Seasonal variations (S) are within-year variations which tend to be much the same year after year. The causes may be natural (such as weather), they may be associated with the calendar, or occur simply as a result of traditions, habits and customs of doing business.

Secular trends (T) are changes in the level of the series over relatively long time periods. While the causes are particular to any series, examples of the forces at work might be changes in population size and/or composition, technological advances, etc.

Cyclical fluctuations (C) are those expansions and contractions, usually more than a year in length, which characterize most time series in business and economics. Some series seem to have cycles which may be described by some simple mathematical construction, such as a sine wave. Most of the actual cycles which have been observed are difficult to characterize except by complex mathematical formulations, as they are quite diverse in amplitude and/or frequency.

Irregular fluctuations (I) are all those which may not be classified as trend, seasonal, or cyclical. The causes are unique events, such as strikes, fires, wars, and other unusual occurrences.

Of course, the forecaster does not have all the components separated for him. There is only the resultant time series, which he presumes is made up of the components. The forecaster must decide whether the combination of the components is additive and/or multiplicative, and then decide on the process for decomposition. The models under consideration here are entirely multiplicative and may be represented by[1]

$$X = S \times T \times C \times I \qquad (2\text{--}10)$$

The series which resulted from the combined forces is represented by X. Since the model assumes that the resultant series is a multiplicative combination of the components, decomposition is obviously by division. Detailed descriptions of the computations will not be given here, nor are they needed because of the availability of computer programs. However, an overview of the computations is given below.

The computations begin with a ratio-to-moving-average procedure to smooth the original series. That is, a 12-month, centered, moving average is computed from $S \times T \times C \times I$. A moving average of a time series is an average computed by sequentially dropping the earliest observed data point and adding the latest observed data point. For example, a three-period moving average of the following series is computed as shown in Table 2–2.

Two aspects of a moving average can be seen from this example. One is that averages cannot be obtained at the beginning and end of the series. This means that a lag is introduced. Second, the averages in this odd numbered moving average are centered in the middle of the time period in question. However, if there were a two, four, or other even number

---

[1] The reader should remember that the subscripts on each of the components have been dropped for simplicity. The more correct notation would be

$$X_{ij} = S_{ij} \times T_{ij} \times C_{ij} \times I_{ij}$$

where $i = 1, \ldots, n$, depending on the number of years in the series and $j = 1, \ldots, 12$ if monthly data are used, $j = 1, \ldots, 4$ if quarterly data, etc.

TABLE 2–2

COMPUTATION OF 3 PERIOD MOVING AVERAGE

Data	Moving Total	$\dfrac{\text{Moving Total}}{3}$ = Moving Average
1.............. 17		
2.............. 19		19.7
3.............. 23	59	22.3
4.............. 25	67	24.0
5.............. 24	72	26.3
6.............. 30	79	

of periods, the average would be centered between periods. In order to center an even numbered moving average, a two-period moving average of the uncentered moving average is computed.

The ratios of the original series to the moving average are then computed and used to smooth the original series for $S \times I$, the resulting series is $T \times C$. The "seasonal-irregular" series is then isolated by division of the original series by $T \times C$.

$$\frac{S \times T \times C \times I}{T \times C} = S \times I \qquad (2\text{--}11)$$

Weighted moving averages of the $S \times I$ series are then used to remove the irregular components. The seasonal component is the remaining series. These seasonals are then converted to an index such that the average monthly value of the index is 1.000 or 100.0, depending on the particular computer program used. Dividing the original series by the seasonal index gives a series free of seasonal fluctuations.

$$\frac{S \times T \times C \times I}{S} = T \times C \times I \qquad (2\text{--}12)$$

Updated seasonal factors are provided to the forecaster each time the programs are run so that he may use the factors to adjust newly received data. This procedure may be useful in giving the forecaster preliminary insight into future changes which the data are beginning to reveal.

The irregular component is also separately identified by the programs. Thus, the forecaster will have at his disposal estimates of seasonal and irregular components, a trend-cycle series, and the final seasonally adjusted series, which is the cycle-irregular series. The program also gives a measure of the average duration of run for some of the components. The run of series is how long it moves in one direction without changing. An average of this characteristic may be of some help in predicting changes in direction.

Armed with the above information, the forecaster is prepared to estimate where the series will go next. He can begin with the present level of the series. Adjustments up or down for the seasonal, cyclical, and trend components are easily made. Since he has duration-of-run information on some of the components, the forecaster has some idea of whether to expect a turning point. Although it violates the strict notion of a naïve model, the forecaster may want to apply some judgmental factors as well.

Link-Relative Models. In the use of link-relative models, the forecaster is attempting to predict changes in a time series rather than the level of the variable in question. The level of a time series at a point in time is highly correlated with the level in the previous time period, so the level of the series is no problem; however, changes may be. In later chapters, models which deal with causes of changes in the level of a variable will be considered. The present technique attempts to forecast a change on the basis of observed past changes only and thus is a naïve technique.

The forecaster must decide whether he is interested in forecasting absolute changes or relative changes. Absolute changes or first differences will be discussed below in the chapters on regression analysis. The percentage or ratio change is of interest with link-relative models.

The procedure is straightforward. The ratio of month-to-month changes is computed for all pairs of successive months. For example,

$$\frac{X_{\text{April}}}{X_{\text{March}}} = \frac{291}{367} = .793$$

is the ratio for the indicated months in Year 6 of Table 2–1. The forecaster must then decide what is the most representative value of this ratio from the array of ratios computed. For some purposes, a simple arithmetic average may serve well. In some instances, it would be useful to compute a geometric average, such as

$$\sqrt[4]{\frac{X_{\text{Feb}}}{X_{\text{Jan}}} \times \frac{X_{\text{Mar}}}{X_{\text{Feb}}} \times \frac{X_{\text{April}}}{X_{\text{Mar}}} \times \frac{X_{\text{May}}}{X_{\text{April}}}}$$

$$= \sqrt[4]{\frac{298}{305} \times \frac{367}{298} \times \frac{291}{367} \times \frac{334}{291}}$$

$$= \sqrt[4]{.977 \times 1.232 \times .793 \times 1.148}$$

$$= 1.023$$

for as many pairs of months as are available. Since small changes are more likely than big changes, the distribution of ratios is likely to be skewed. Thus, a median or modal value might be chosen. The ultimate choice is up to the forecaster after he has examined the data and decided which will be most representative, given his data.

For some purposes, a single value for the link-relative model, be it mean, median or mode, will not be relevant. If there is a strong seasonal pattern in the data, then improved forecasts may be prepared by taking, say, a median over the same pair of months for as many years as are available. Thus twelve ratios would be computed and the appropriate one used to prepare any particular forecast.

It would also be possible to compute a measure of dispersion for the distribution of ratios observed. Thus, the forecaster would prepare a point forecast and also put confidence limits on the forecast.[2] Or, if computed measures of dispersion seem inappropriate, then subjective confidence limits could be generated and a range of possible outcomes forecast.

Although the above discussion has run in terms of monthly changes, there is no reason why the technique could not be applied to other time periods for which data are available. As longer time periods are considered, it is necessary to indicate a greater degree of uncertainty by placing wider confidence limits on the forecast.

Exponential Smoothing. Exponential smoothing or adaptive forecasting uses a weighted moving average of past data as the basis for a forecast. The weights are a geometric progression with smaller weights assigned to observations in the more distant past. Thus the procedure gives heaviest weight to more recent information and discounts the distant past more heavily. Of course the procedure is amenable to computer usage, and adjustments for seasonal patterns and trends are possible.

It is convenient to start with a geometric series of the following sort:

$$1, (1 - \alpha), (1 - \alpha)^2, (1 - \alpha)^3, \ldots\ldots, (1 - \alpha)^{n-1} \quad (2\text{--}13)$$

Each number in this series is progressively smaller for values of α between zero and one. For a simple example, let α take on the value of $\frac{1}{2}$. The series becomes

$$1, \tfrac{1}{2}, \tfrac{1}{4}, \tfrac{1}{8}, \ldots\ldots, (\tfrac{1}{2})^{n-1} \quad (2\text{--}14)$$

The terms of such a series could be used as weights in the computation of a weighted moving average of a time series

---

[2] A point forecast is an attempt to make a precise estimate of the forecast variable. The probability of being exactly correct is essentially zero. Hence, a forecast that the observed value will lie within a certain range with a specified probability may be much more useful.

giving the most recent data the largest weight. The average would be computed by

$$\overline{X}_t = \frac{1X_t + (1-\alpha)X_{t-1} + (1-\alpha)^2 X_{t-2} + \cdots \cdots + (1-\alpha)^{n-1}X_{t-(n-1)}}{1 + (1-\alpha) + (1-\alpha)^2 + \cdots \cdots + (1-\alpha)^{n-1}} \quad (2\text{-}15)$$

The resulting moving average, $\overline{X}_t$, gives a smoothed estimate of the value of X in period t, using all observed values of X weighted by the exponentially declining weights of the geometric series.

It is useful to consider how this moving average changes as new observations on X become available. For example, in period $t + 1$, it becomes

$$\overline{X}_{t+1} = \alpha[X_{t+1} + (1-\alpha)X_t + (1-\alpha)^2 X_{t-1} + \cdots \cdots + (1-\alpha)^{n-1}X_{t-(n-2)}] \quad (2\text{-}16)$$

A comparison of the expressions for $\overline{X}_{t+1}$ and $\overline{X}_t$ yields an interesting observation. This is most easily seen if the expression for $\overline{X}_t$ is multiplied through by the constant $(1-\alpha)$. Equation (2–15) becomes

$$(1-\alpha)\overline{X}_t = \alpha[(1-\alpha)X_t + (1-\alpha)^2 X_{t-1} + (1-\alpha)^3 X_{t-2} + \cdots + (1-\alpha)^n X_{t-(n-1)}] \quad (2\text{-}17)$$

The term to the right of the equals sign in Equation (2–17) is the same as the right-hand side of Equation (2–16) with one term missing. Thus, addition of the missing term, αX_{t+1}, to Equation (2–17) gives us Equation (2–18) in much simplified form:

$$\overline{X}_{t+1} = \alpha X_{t+1} + (1-\alpha)\overline{X}_t \quad (2\text{-}18)$$

This is a very useful observation. Once an exponentially weighted, smoothed, moving average of a time series has been computed, it may be updated easily, since all that is needed is the last exponentially weighted average, $(\overline{X}_t)$, the constant term (α), and the new observation. Notice that the oldest observations in the series are retained, though they are given lesser weight. Rewriting Equation (2–2) to make it apply to current observations, we obtain Equation (2–19).

$$\overline{X}_t = \alpha X_t + (1 - \alpha)\overline{X}_{t-1} \qquad (2\text{–}19)$$

Then the forecast becomes

$$\hat{X}_{t+1} = \overline{X}_t$$

which is the latest smoothed value of X.

The above forecast may be very satisfactory for series which exhibit neither seasonality nor trend. It is possible to incorporate corrections for both, but, before we turn to such additions, it is necessary to consider the estimation of the value of the constant terms. In the above discussion, α was assumed to have a value somewhere between zero and one. The larger the value of α, the more weight is given to current or recent data.

The usual method of estimating the value of α is an iterative procedure. Formally the problem may be stated

$$\min \sum_{t=1}^{n} (\hat{X}_t - X_t)^2 \qquad (2\text{–}20)$$

where n is the number of observations available. The forecasts are computed for α equal to $0.1, 0.2, \ldots, 0.9$, and the sum of the squared forecast errors is computed. This first trial may indicate the 0.6 and 0.7 are about equally good values for α. The procedure would then be repeated for α equal to 0.61, 0.62, $\ldots, 0.69$, and the sums of the squared forecasts errors would again be computed. The value of α producing the smallest error would then be chosen.

Seasonal and trend factors may be added in the following way. The adjustment factors are also computed as exponentially smoothed estimates and need their own smoothing weights. Forecasters using such techniques usually recompute the estimates of the various constants or weights from time to time but not too often, as the iterative process becomes quite lengthy.

As an example, the following ratio or multiplicative trend adjustment will be added. A similar approach is possible with a seasonal adjustment. The smoothing equation becomes

$$\hat{X}_t = \alpha X_t + (1 \times \alpha) R_t \bar{X}_{t-1} \qquad (2\text{-}19)$$

where the notation remains as above with the addition of the term R_t, which is the trend adjustment. More precisely, R_t is the estimate of $\bar{X}_t / \bar{X}_{t-1}$, which implies a trend of constant percentage change.

The estimate of R_t is obtained as an exponentially smoothed weighted average of the current observed ratio and all past ratios, as follows

$$R_t = c \, \frac{\bar{X}_t}{\bar{X}_{t-1}} + (1 - c) \, \bar{R}_{t-1} \qquad (2\text{-}20)$$

The computations are such that R_t and $\bar{X}_t$ are simultaneously determined. Substituting Equation (2-20) into Equation (2-19) gives

$$\bar{X}_t = \frac{\alpha}{1 - (1 - \alpha)c} \, X_t + \frac{(1 - \alpha)(1 - c)}{1 - (1 - \alpha)c} \bar{R}_{t-1} \, \bar{X}_{t-1} \quad (2\text{-}21)$$

in which all terms are known. Estimates of α and c are determined by the same procedure as for α alone, with the process becoming more complex.

An estimate of R_t to be used for the next period may be obtained by substitution of Equation (2-21) back into Equation (2-20).

$$R_t = \frac{\alpha \, c}{1 - (1 - \alpha)c} \, \frac{X_t}{\bar{X}_{t-1}} + \frac{1 - c}{1 - (1 - \alpha)c} \, \bar{R}_{t-1}$$

The forecast, using R_t from Equation (2-21), becomes

$$\hat{X}_{t+T} = \bar{X}_t R_t^{\,T} \quad (T = 1, 2, \ldots, M) \qquad (2\text{-}22)$$

where T is the number of periods ahead for which the forecast is being made. Because of the compound growth assumption, this method should not be used for large M, where M is the number of periods to be forecast.

Without all the algebra the seasonal adjustment alone may be performed or a seasonal and trend adjustment combined. An example of the combination would be

$$\bar{X}_t = \alpha X_t S_t + (1 - \alpha) R_t \bar{X}_{t-1} \qquad (2\text{-}23)$$

By a process similar to the one described above, the following estimating equations may be obtained:

$$\bar{X}_t = \left[\frac{\alpha(1 - \beta)}{1 - \alpha\beta - (1 - \alpha)c} \right] X_t S_{t-N}$$
$$+ \left[\frac{(1 - \alpha)(1 - c)}{1 - \alpha\beta - (1 - \alpha)c} \right] \bar{X}_{t-1} R_{t-1} \quad (2\text{-}24)$$

$$S_t = \left[\frac{[1 - \beta][1 - (1 - \alpha)c]}{1 - \alpha\beta - (1 - \alpha)c} \right] S_{t-N}$$
$$+ \left[\frac{\beta(1 - \alpha)(1 - c)}{1 - \alpha\beta - (1 - \alpha)c} \right] \frac{\bar{X}_{t-1}}{X_t} R_{t-1} \quad (2\text{-}25)$$

$$R_t = \left[\frac{\alpha\, c(1 - \beta)}{1 - \alpha\beta - (1 - \alpha)c} \right] \frac{X_t S_{t-N}}{\bar{X}_{t-1}}$$
$$+ \left[\frac{(1 - c)(1 - \alpha\beta)}{1 - \alpha\beta - (1 - \alpha)\, c} \right] R_{t-1} \quad (2\text{-}26)$$

The constants α, β, and c are the exponential smoothing weights for the raw series and for the seasonal and trend adjustments, respectively. The variable S_t is the seasonal adjustment factor, and S_{t-N} is the last known seasonal factor for the relevant time period. All other notation remains the same. The forecast becomes

$$\hat{X}_{t+T} = \frac{\bar{X}_t R_t^T}{S_{t+T-N}} \quad T = 1, 2, \ldots, M \qquad (2\text{-}27)$$

REFERENCES

Box, G. E. P. *Time Series, Forecasting, and Control.* San Francisco: Holden-Day, 1968.

————, and G. M. Jenkins. *Time-Series Analysis, Forecasting, and Control.* San Francisco: Holden-Day, 1968.

Muth, J. F. "Optimal Properties of Exponentially Weighted Forecasts." *Journal of the American Statistical Association,* Vol. LV, 1960, pp. 299–306.

Packer, A. H. "Simulation and Adaptive Forecasting as Applied to Inventory Control." *Journal of the Operations Research Society,* Vol. XV, July–August, 1967.

Parzen, E. *Empirical Time-Series Analysis.* San Francisco: Holden-Day, 1969.

————. *Time-Series Analysis Papers.* San Francisco: Holden-Day, 1967.

Robinson, E. A. *Multi-Channel Time-Series Analysis with Digital Computer Programs.* San Francisco: Holden-Day, 1967.

Salzman, L. *Computerized Economic Analysis.* New York: McGraw-Hill, 1968.

Shiskin, J., and H. Eisenpress. "Seasonal Adjustments by Electronic Computer Methods." *Journal of the American Statistical Association,* Vol. LII, December, 1957, pp. 415–49.

"Summary Description of X-9 and X-10 Versions of the Census Method II Seasonal Adjustment Program." *Business Cycle Developments,* September, 1963.

U.S. Bureau of Labor Statistics. *The BLS Seasonal Factor Method: Its Application by Electronic Computer,* June, 1963.

Young, A. "Linear Approximations to the Census and BLS Seasonal Adjustment Methods." *Journal of the American Statistical Association,* Vol. LXIII, June, 1968.

chapter
—3—
Survey Methods of Forecasting

Next, our discussion turns to several widely used forecasting models which are neither naïve nor structural, though there may be elements of both involved. Inclusion of these models at this point should not lead to the conclusion that the models are in some sense intermediate between naïve and structural, though "opportunistic" forecasts are in the middle to the extent that many techniques are combined.

The most obvious way to find out what people are going to do is to ask them. While this technique may be applied almost anywhere, the best known surveys are in business fixed investment and consumer durables. A number of survey methods will be considered in this chapter. Such models are not naïve, since no past data enter; and, while a structural model is implied, no attempt is made to discover what the structure may be.

Another widely known technique is usually called the "barometric" approach and makes use of indicators of business activity. Barometric models which will be discussed in the next chapter, are close to naïve models, in that past time series are used. The difference is that a combination of time series is used to forecast yet other time series. Further, there is an implicit "business cycles" model serving as underpinning for the technique.

Chapter 5 will include a discussion of "opportunistic" forecasting. Naïve models are suggestive of this approach, since the forecaster develops his sources of information by whatever means seem reasonable. Thus, elements of naïve, survey, and structural forecasts may all contribute to the final forecast. John Lewis has long used the opportunistic approach in preparing his GNP forecasts, and a short sketch of his model will be given below.

POLLS OR SURVEY TECHNIQUES

Surveys of intentions to buy exist for two major sectors of the economy. Since these sectors are important from a theoretical point of view and frequently are volatile in performance, it is fortunate for the forecaster that surveys do exist. The sectors surveyed are 1) business plant and equipment and 2) consumer expenditures. The consumer surveys focus on some "big ticket" durable items, but attitudes concerning purchases are also surveyed.

1. BUSINESS PLANT AND EQUIPMENT SURVEYS

The categories of business plant and equipment expenditures surveyed are much narrower in scope than the concept of business fixed investment in the gross private domestic investment GNP expenditure account. Thus the forecaster attempting to forecast GNP needs to produce separate estimates of the other components of investment. These other components are capital expenditures by nonprofit institutions, farm construction and equipment expenditures, and business capital expenditures which have been charged to current expense accounts by corporations. The forecaster for a firm producing business plant and equipment items must still decide how a change in the survey will be translated into sales changes for his firm. Despite this, accurate surveys of business plant and equipment are available and are quite useful to forecasters.

Business fixed investment consists of nonresidential structures and producer durables. The statistical series of past expenditures may be readily separated into farm and nonfarm segments, but further breakdowns are more difficult. The survey results are not readily reconcilable with the national income accounts definition of business fixed investment, though the difference may not be troublesome for most uses since the changes in the two data series are highly correlated. The difference between the survey and the GNP figures may be estimated by simple projection techniques.

Commerce-SEC. The U.S. Department of Commerce-Securities and Exchange Commission survey is published quarterly in the *Survey of Current Business*. While the sample is by no means large, it is larger and more comprehensive than the McGraw-Hill survey discussed below. Because of the timing of publication, many forecasters use the two surveys together in order to gain the most insights possible.

The Commerce-SEC survey is published in the third month of each quarter. With each issue, a revised estimate of expenditures for the current quarter and the survey results for the next quarter are published. In December the estimate for the second quarter of the next calendar year is included. The March issue contains the estimate for the calendar year, by then three months gone. With the yearly estimate, the revised first-quarter estimate, and the second-quarter estimate, the forecaster can project the expenditures for the last half of the calendar year.

McGraw-Hill. The McGraw-Hill survey, published twice a year in *Business Week,* is also very useful, though the nature of the sample makes it susceptible to error when business activity changes direction. By concentrating on large firms in order to pick up the big capital-expenditure programs, this survey misses the smaller firms, which are more likely to be sensitive to short-run changes in business conditions and to revise their investment plans.

The preliminary survey is taken early in the fourth quarter and released early in November. This is late enough that most firms have pretty well fixed their expenditures for the following year. This release date is perfect for the forecaster preparing his forecast for the following calendar year.

A resurvey is taken in the spring of the year and published in April. The results of this survey are usually very accurate, as most business budgets are by then operational, subject to no further review unless there is a substantial change in economic conditions. Both the fall and the spring surveys contain forecasts for more than a year ahead. The past predictive accuracy of these longer term surveys has been considerably less reliable than the annual surveys.

Because of the pattern of quarterly publication of the Commerce-SEC survey and the twice-yearly publication of the McGraw-Hill survey, it is easy to see how the forecaster can use both to keep his estimate of investment expenditures up to date. Of course, to get an estimate which is consistent with the national income accounts definition of business fixed investment, the forecaster will need to project proportionately the appropriate values for farm, nonprofit institutions, and oil-well drilling.

Both surveys are now asking additional information which serves as internal checks on the firmness and validity of the responses. While other questions may be asked from time to time, basically three items of additional information are sought. They are: (1) Do expenditure plans allow for changes in the price of capital goods; (2) What is the firm's own forecast of sales or GNP; and, (3) What are its present and preferred rates of capacity utilization.

National Industrial Conference Board.   Another useful survey, also available quarterly, is the survey of capital appropriations carried out by the National Industrial Conference Board. A capital appropriation is a commitment by a firm's board of directors to make a capital outlay, usually in the near-term future. The survey results are published in the Board's own publications and in the *Survey of Current Business*. When using this survey, the forecaster must be aware that the data refer to a sample of 1000 manufacturing firms, not all firms. However, this sample does account for a substantial percentage of the total capital expenditures in the economy. The survey picks up plans which are reasonably firm and for which appropriations have been made, though the date of expenditure is not clear. Of course, this survey would miss those definitely planned expenditures for which appropriations have not been made. Nevertheless, the survey results might be quite useful to firms selling primarily to manufacturers—and it has been of particular help in picking up turning points in the plant and equipment series.

Fortune.   It is worth noting that *Fortune* magazine publishes surveys of capital expenditure plans from time to time. Irregular availability reduces their otherwise acceptable usefulness as a tool of the forecaster

Final Comment

The forecaster may want to make further adjustments, but such actions are a matter of personal taste and the forecaster's own ability to sense changes in the economy. One cross-check on the intentions surveys is the operating rate of industries producing the investment goods relative to their capacity. The industry may be unable to produce all the capital goods that investors would like to purchase. Most forecasters do not worry about short-run changes in sales or the interest rate, since investment plans are affected by such changes only with a substantial lag, often up to a year. Thus, it is common practice to assume that most of these side issues were considered by the respondents to the survey and to accept the results of the survey as a reliable estimate.

2. CONSUMER DURABLES SURVEYS

The surveys of consumers' intentions to buy have not enjoyed the same success as the surveys of business-expenditures intentions. Part of the reason is that most people don't carefully plan their purchases, even for "big ticket" items. Further, households are more vulnerable to economic uncertainties than are businesses. Another part of the difficulty arises from the nature of the surveys themselves. A discussion of their weaknesses and some suggestions for improvement follow a discussion of some of the well-known surveys of consumers.

Available Surveys

In addition to the following listing which is not intended to be exhaustive but does include many of the best known surveys, there are many private surveys. Most private surveys, however, tend to be confidential and unavailable to others, or to relate to marketing of specific products—thus they are not usually of general interest or usefulness.

Survey Research Center, University of Michigan. One of the best known surveys is that of the Survey Research Center of the University of Michigan. From its inception this survey has attempted to measure consumer intentions to buy durable goods, mostly cars and major appliances. Some information on consumer asset positions and savings plans is also gathered.

While the Center continues to obtain the above information, interest in recent years has shifted to more subtle questioning to determine consumers' attitudes on their financial well-being and job security, their willingness to spend, and their desire to save.

Albert Sindlinger Co. This is a private survey which is generally available. The source is *Business Record,* a publication of the National Industrial Conference Board.

Consumers Union. This survey is conducted each year by Consumers Union. The respondents are its subscriber-members. While the information may be very good for the sample, subscribers to *Consumer Reports* are not representative of the society as a whole. Thus it is difficult to use the information in forecasting market performance.

U.S. Bureau of the Census. The results of the Census survey are published in *Current Population Reports* as series P-65, "Consumer Buying Indications." This survey will be discussed more fully below.

Commercial Credit Company. The Commercial Credit Company of Baltimore has recently begun publishing a quarterly pamphlet, *Consumer Buying Prospects,* which contains the census data mentioned above plus some interpretation of the data. One of the editors of the publication is Thomas Juster, whose contribution to consumer surveys will be discussed in the following paragraphs.

Consumer Surveys: Strengths and Weaknesses [1]

Attempts to use historical relationships between purchases of consumer durables and such other variables as income,

---

[1] This discussion follows F. Thomas Juster, *Consumer Buying Intentions and Purchase Probability,* Occasional Paper 99, National Bureau of Economic Research (New York: Columbia University Press, 1966). Basically the same article appeared in *Journal of the American Statistical Association,* September, 1966.

wealth, liquidity, prices, and/or interest rates as a means of forecasting future sales of consumer durables have failed miserably. The obvious solution was to ask consumers about their purchase intentions. Such an approach should work, since "big ticket" durable items are not usually bought on impulse. However, surveys have not been very successful in the past. Reflection should reveal the shortcomings.

Surveys tended to use a variant of the question, "Do you plan (expect, intend) to buy a (insert name of durable good) during the next 6, 12, 18, 24 months?" The response might well be a ten minute discourse, especially if the lady of the house was the respondent. However, the interviewer is limited to recording a single word response, such as "definitely," "probably," "don't know," or "no." A follow-up survey records actual purchases. In addition to projecting sales rates directly from the responses, the analyst also watches each category of response for changes over time in the actual purchase rate reported. Cross-sectionally, the analyst watches for shifts in purchase rates of intenders and nonintenders.

To illustrate the difficulty with such an approach, Juster uses the following example. An interviewer approaches a respondent during April and asks him about his intentions to take a vacation during the summer. The respondent, at that time, is unlikely to have a specific date or definite plans for a vacation, though he is quite certain that he will take a vacation of some sort during the summer. If the respondent says he expects to take a vacation, a "yes" response is recorded. But "plan" to vacation elicits a "no" response, as plans are not formed. And "intend" to vacation elicits a "don't know" response—since, taken literally, the intention to vacation *come what may* is seldom found in anybody. Yet the respondent might very well be able to indicate that the chances are nine out of ten that he will take a vacation. This possibility of obtaining probabalistic information leads directly to Juster's study.

Juster felt that two testable hypotheses might be distilled from the literature on surveys. First, statements by respondents about buying intentions are really probability statements in disguise. Thus, a survey should be devised which would strip away the disguises. The second is a corrollary of the first, to wit: a survey of explicit purchase probabilities would yield a superior forecast of future purchase rates.

To test the hypothesis about probability statements, the regular respondents in the "Quarterly Survey of Intentions by Census" were asked to answer the questions then in use and then to choose a statement which most closely described what they meant by their answer. The list was as follows:

Descriptive Word	Probability
certain, practically certain	.99
almost sure	.9
very probable	.8
probable	.7
good possibility	.6
fairly good possibility	.5
fair possibility	.4
some possibility	.3
slight possibility	.2
very slight possibility	.1
no chance, almost no chance	.01

The results were quite interesting. The probability scale and the intentions scale gave quite different results. Many nonintenders reported probabilities of purchase greater than zero. And about 10 percent of the "don't know" responses gave probabilities greater than zero. This response pattern is not inconsistent. It is possible not to know whether you will buy a car and yet have a positive prior probability on the necessity of replacing your old one. Similarly, it is possible that one would not intend to buy a car while conceding that the odds are about even that a teenage son will succeed in talking one into such a purchase.

The hypothesis of superior forecasting using probabilities is thus sustained, and since 1966 the Bureau of the Census has been conducting regular quarterly surveys using the probability responses. The data published under the title *Consumer Buying Indicators* is obtained from a random sample of approximately 15,000 households representing all fifty states and the District of Columbia. The full sample comprises six independent subsamples (rotation groups) of approximately 2,500 households each. About 83.3 percent of the sample households are thus identical in consecutive surveys. This procedure tends to minimize sampling error in the measurement of changes. The results of the survey for automobiles are shown in Table 3–1.

Juster noted, and census data confirms, that the actual purchase rate exceeds the mean reported probability. That is, simple projection of sales from the responses results in a fore-

TABLE 3–1

Mean Probabilities of Buying Cars
(average number of chances in 100)

	1968				1969
	January	*April*	*July*	*October*	*January*
Within 6 months:					
Any.....................	9.4	9.8	9.6	8.9	9.0
New....................	4.4	4.5	4.8	4.6	4.3
Used..................	4.6	4.8	4.3	3.8	4.2
Type not specified........	.4	.5	.5	.5	.5
Within 12 months:					
Any.	18.4	18.5	18.8	18.3	18.0
New.........	9.4	9.3	10.0	9.9	9.4
Used.	8.0	8.1	7.6	7.4	7.6
Type not specified...... .	1.0	1.1	1.2	1.0	1.0
Within 24 months:					
Any.....................	33.5	33.6	32.8	32.8	32.5
New..................	18.3	18.1	18.4	18.6	18.0
Used..................	13.2	13.2	12.2	12.3	12.4
Type not specified........	2.0	2.3	2.2	1.9	2.1

cast that is only 65 percent of the actual purchase rate. To overcome this downward bias, we can prepare the forecast in the following manner. We compute an index number by the following technique:

1. Develop a weighted 6-month mean probability by adding twice the mean probability of buying a new car within 6 months to the mean probability of buying within 6 months a used car and a car of unspecified type.

2. Add twice the weighted 6-month mean probability (the result in number 1) from the current survey to the weighted 6-month mean probability from the preceding survey.

3. Multiply the results in number 2 by an index of households to account for household growth.

4. The 6-month index value for a given quarter is the quarter's results from number 3 divided by the average of the results from number 3 for January 1967, and April 1967.

5. Repeat as above, using mean probabilities of buying within 12 months to derive a 12-month index value.

6. Average the 6- and 12-month index values to get the final index of expected car purchases.

The relationship between the level of the index and household purchases of automobiles is then estimated by a regression analysis. The equation as estimated for the first half of 1969 is

$$\text{Purchases} = 5.330.5 + 89.7 \text{ Index} + 191.4 \text{ Strike}$$
$$(29.1) \qquad (136.4)$$
$$s_{yx} = 192.3 \quad \bar{R}^2 = .76$$

The figures in parentheses represent the standard errors of the coefficients, and

Purchases = number of new cars reported purchased by households during the next 2 quarters (in thousands).

Index = the value of the index of expected new-car purchases at the beginning of a 2-quarter period. This index is calculated as shown above.

Strike = a dummy variable equal to -1 for the period including the third and fourth quarters of 1967 and equal to $+1$ for the period including the first and second quarters of 1968. It is equal to zero other times. This variable is included to account for the disparity between anticipations and purchases resulting from supply shortages caused by the strike in September and October, 1967.

The index at the start of 1969 was 101.7. The forecast becomes

$$P = -5.330.5 + 89.7(101.7) + 191.4(0)$$
$$= 3791.99$$

for the first quarter, which is roughly 7.6 million units for the first half of 1969.

While such attempts to upgrade intentions surveys have certainly improved the nature of the results, much is yet to be learned. The probability-survey technique has been in use since mid-1966, but forecasts are available only from 1968 on. More experience is certainly required.

Other difficulties must also be considered. The census taker will accept any adult of the household as a respondent, and this person may not be the person who ultimately makes the purchase decision. Also, the respondent may be unable to state accurately his purchase expectations. Juster has suggested the priming of the respondent by an initial review of family financial characteristics.

The stated probability of purchase is as of a moment in time. Changes in family circumstances may alter the purchase probability. However, to the extent that such mishaps are random, the forecast need not be invalidated. On the other hand, changes in general economic conditions will not be random, and the impact of these changes must be assessed by the forecaster. Further, changes on the supply side must be anticipated, and considerations of industry capacity, pricing policy, and labor relations may influence actual purchases made.

Finally, as an extension of the probability-of-purchase survey, Theil and Kosobud suggest that, by using the concepts of information theory, the analyst may improve his estimates of probability of purchase.[2] Without developing the method suggested, the procedures of information analysis allow the analyst to combine his surveys of prior probabilities of purchase and the "information" obtained by the follow-up surveys of actual purchases to improve still further his estimates of purchase of consumer durables.

REFERENCES

ADAMS, F. GERARD. "Prediction with Consumer Attitudes: The Time Series–Cross Section Paradox." *The Review of Economics and Statistics,* November, 1965.

JUSTER, F. THOMAS. *Anticipations and Purchases: An Analysis of Consumer Behavior.* Princeton University Press for National Bureau of Economic Research, 1964.

KATONA, GEORGE. *The Powerful Consumer.* New York, 1964.

MINCER, JACOB (ed.). *Economic Forecasts and Expectations.* National Bureau of Economic Research, 1969.

MUELLER, EVA. "Effects of Consumer Attitudes on Purchases." *American Economic Review,* December, 1957.

———. "Ten Years of Consumer Attitude Surveys: Their Forecasting Record." *Journal of the American Statistical Association,* December, 1963.

OKUN, ARTHUR. "The Value of Anticipations Data in Forecasting National Product." *The Quality and Economic Significance of Anticipations Data,* Princeton University Press for National Bureau of Economic Research, 1960.

TOBIN, JAMES. "On the Predictive Value of Consumer Intentions and Attitudes." *Review of Economics and Statistics,* February, 1959.

---

[2] Theil, H., and Kosobud, R. F., "How Informative Are Consumer Buying Intentions Surveys?" *Review of Economics and Statistics,* Vol. XLX, February 1968.

chapter
—4—
Barometric or Indicator Forecasts

It has long been recognized that if it were possible to identify, out of the mass of economic data available, one or more time series which always gave correct indications of the future, much of the forecaster's work would be completed. In the literature growing out of the search for such a series, such names as Arthur Burns, Geoffrey Moore, Wesley Mitchell, and Julius Shiskin may be found. While some of the research goes back some distance in time, the present format of business-cycle data dates from the late 1950s, when the Council of Economic Advisers became interested in using the technology of time-series analysis and in making the data available to others. The National Bureau of Economic Research and the Bureau of Census cooperated to develop the data and techniques, and *Business Conditions Digest*.[1] The data described below are to be found in this publication. Our discussion describes the data after the 1966 revisions and the newly adopted scoring plan for choosing the series to be used.

---

[1] This monthly publication was begun in October 1961 as *Business Cycle Development*.

ECONOMIC INDICATORS

Economic indicators are sensitive series which tend to turn up or down in advance of, concurrent with, or after other series of interest. Figure 4–1 illustrates the concept underlying the use of indicators. The vertical lines indicate the peak and trough date of a cycle which has been identified.

FIGURE 4–1

Economic Indicators Illustrated

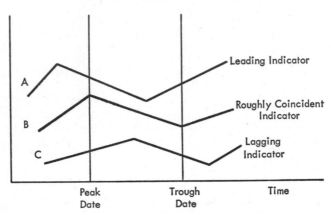

Line *A* shows a leading indicator, that is, a series which reaches its peak in advance of the peak of the general cycle peak. A roughly coincident indicator is illustrated by line *B*. The lagging indicator shown in line *C* peaks after the peak of the general cycle.

WHY TWO LISTS?

It would be very convenient if there were a single series or a very small number of series which would infallibly predict future business activity. Since this is not the case, additional series must be used and a larger view of the problem encompassed. However, if no selectivity is practiced, the analyst is confronted with the whole confusing mass of information. Thus, while the final selection may in part be arbitrary, careful analysis has shown that some series are better than others from the analyst's point of view. Once a group of series has been chosen, sometimes the entire set may be used while at other times only a subset may be used. The reasons are as follows.

Two lists of economic indicators are regularly available for use by the analyst. The full list includes 88 U.S. series: 36 leading, 25 roughly coincident, and 16 unclassified by timing. Of these series, 72 are monthly and 16 quarterly. The short list includes 25 U.S. series: 12 leading, 7 coincident, and 6 lagging. There is little economic sector duplication on this list of 21 monthly and 4 quarterly series, all of which are included in the long list.

To the extent that choices can be made—the fewer time series used, the easier it will be to summarize, communicate, and comprehend the information which the analyst obtains from the data. Thus, there is clearly a gain in using the short list, though there is just as clearly a loss of detail. Further, as presently constituted the short list contains primarily series which are available monthly, giving it the additional advantage of more up-to-date analysis of events.

On the other hand, the long list contains series which are too valuable for analysts to ignore, yet which suffer from defects which preclude them from the shorter list. For example, some economically significant series may have no consistent pattern of timing with respect to the business cycle. Government receipts and expenditures and foreign trade fall into this category. Similarly a series which does not go far enough in time to gather cycle experience may yet be valuable on other grounds. Duplication in the long list provides some possible benefits. Some series appear more frequently and may be more timely than other more conceptually appropriate series. Others may have incomplete coverage but more sharply defined cyclical variability. Having closely related series available allows crosschecking which cannot be accomplished otherwise. Thus the choice of more timely availability in the use of the short versus the long list depends on the analyst and the problem which he has at hand.

The Long List

To further facilitate analysis, the long list is subdivided a number of ways. The only division of interest here is the classification by economic process. For the analyst interested in a particular segment of the economy, this classification should be particularly useful. The categories are

Economic Process	Number of Series
Employment, unemployment	14
Production, income, consumption, trade	8
Fixed capital investment	14
Inventories, inventory investment	9
Prices, costs, profits	11
Money, credit	17
Foreign trade, payments	6
Federal government activity	9
Economic activity in other countries	7

In turn, each of the economic-process categories is further subdivided. For example, the employment and unemployment category contains five groupings: marginal employment adjustment, job vacancies, comprehensive employment series, comprehensive unemployment series, and long duration unemployment. Each of the subgroups has one to five series. Marginal employment adjustment contains five, all leading: (*a*) Average work week, production workers, manufacturing; (*b*) Nonagricultural placements; (*c*) Accession rates, manufacturing; (*d*) Initial claims, unemployment insurance (inverted); and (*e*) Layoff rate, manufacturing (inverted). Long duration unemployment contains only one, a lagging series entitled Unemployment rate, persons unemployed 15+ weeks (inverted).

The Short List

The series included in the short list are shown in Table 4–1. This current short list is an improvement over the previous (1960) version for three reasons. This list contains fewer series related to manufacturing alone and fewer series with low scores for conformity and/or timing. Only two of the latter type remain. Three brand new series have been added which are thought to be superior to any included previously.

TABLE 4–1

Short List of Indicators: Scores and Timing Characteristics

Classification and Series Title	*First Business Cycle Turn Covered*	*Average Score*	*Median Lead (−) or Lag (+) in Months*
Leading indicators (12 series)			
Average work week, production workers, manufacturing	1921	66	− 5
Nonagricultural, placements, BES	1945	68	− 3
Index of net business formation	1945	68	− 7
New orders, durable goods industries	1920	78	− 4
Contracts and orders, plant and equipment	1948	64	− 6
New building permits, private housing units	1918	67	− 6
Change in book value, manufacturing and trade inventories	1945	65	− 8
Industrial materials prices	1919	67	− 2
Stock prices, 500 common stocks	1873	81	− 4
Corporate profits after taxes, Q	1920	68	− 2
Ratio, price to unit labor cost, manufacturing	1919	69	− 3
Change in consumer installment debt	1929	63	−10

Table 4–1—Continued

Classification and Series Title	First Business Cycle Turn Covered	Average Score	Median Lead (−) or Lag (+) in Months
Roughly coincident indicators (7 series)			
Employees in nonagricultural establishments....................	1929	81	0
Unemployment rate, total (inverted).....	1929	75	0
GNP in constant dollars, expenditures estimate, Q.......................	1921	73	− 2
Industrial production..................	1919	72	0
Personal income.......................	1921	74	− 1
Manufacturing and trade sales...........	1948	71	0
Sales of retail stores....................	1919	69	0
Lagging indicators (6 series)			
Unemployment rate, persons unemployed 15+ weeks (inverted)..............	1948	69	+ 2
Business expenditures plant and equipment, Q........................	1918	86	+ 1
Book value, manufacturing and trade inventories.......................	1945	71	+ 2
Labor cost per unit of output, manufacturing....................	1919	68	+ 8
Commercial and industrial loans outstanding........................	1937		+ 2
Bank rates, short-term business loans, Q.........................	1919	60	+ 5

Source: Moore, G. H. and Shiskin, J., *Indicators of Business Expansions and Contractions* (New York: National Bureau of Economic Research, 1967).

THE SCORING SYSTEM

Out of the literally millions of time series which exist, the analyst is faced with the problem of choosing a limited number which will be useful. In the past the researchers making the choice relied heavily on their own experience and judgment. For the recent revision, a scoring scale was developed in order to aid in the selection process. It does not eliminate the need for decision and choice, but it serves as a rough guide. Further, it is a convenient way for the researchers to account for the factors considered and the weighting scheme used in making their choice.

To give the reader a feel for the process of scoring, we will discuss below the six general areas used in the scoring process. The weights and numerical calculations will be set aside, except for a few summary statistics. Of the many time series considered, 120 were assigned scores. On the basis of 100, the average score was 62, the range 35–89. The average scores for the short list are shown in Table 4–1. As can be seen, the highest-scoring series is not included for other reasons. The six broad categories on which each series was scored are described below.

Economic Significance. In scoring any particular time series, the analyst considers two things. The first is the role given the economic process measured in the various business-cycle theories. Presumably, the more central the role, the higher the score. The second consideration is the breadth of coverage of the series—e.g., manufacturing versus the economy as a whole. The broader the coverage, the more likely a certain amount of averaging takes place so that the series performs well even though various components change, perhaps substantially. But the score is not a simple matter in this case, as narrower coverage might be preferred in some cases precisely in order for specific changes to be picked up.

Statistical Adequacy. There are quite a few criteria for judging the statistical adequacy of a series. A higher score is awarded for meeting each criterion in turn. A series should be based on a reporting system rather than on indirect sources or estimates. The series should have complete coverage or a very good sampling technique. The data should be collected over the entire time period which the series purports to measure. There should be regular provision for revision of preliminary estimates. The series should be naturally smooth or be processed through a seasonal smoothing technique. Finally, there should be good comparability of the series over time.

Conformity. To receive a high score in conformity, the series should have matched past cycles very well. This implies not only the same direction of movement but also roughly similar amplitude. There should also be a *lack* of false turns and/or recent evidence of contrary movements.

Timing. The considerations of timing go beyond the obvious—that is, whether a series always leads, lags, or is coincident with the cycle. To get a higher score in timing, the series should *lack* large variability in length of lead (lag), evidence of missing recent turns, evidence of a long-term shift in length of lead (lag), and/or substantial differences in length of lead (lag) at peaks as compared with troughs.

Currency. The highest score in currency is awarded to the series which is available soonest subject to considerations of accuracy of reporting or need for revision.

Smoothness. A series adjudged worthy of a high score on smoothness is naturally free of irregular and seasonal fluctuations and exhibits well defined cyclical variation.

The various series are scored on each of the six characteristics, and then a weighting procedure is applied to yield the overall score.[2]

USES OF BAROMETRIC TECHNIQUES

Barometric or indicator techniques are useful to the forecaster in predicting the direction of change and turnarounds in business activity. But predicting how far or how fast business

---

[2] A description of the numerical scoring process may be found in Moore & Shiskin, *Indicators of Business Expansions and Contractions,* New York: National Bureau of Economic Research, Columbia University Press, 1967, pp. 8–28.

activity will change is as difficult as any prediction at all when the signals being given are quite mixed. At least *partial solutions* to these problems are discussed below, the latter problem first.

Diffusion Index

The diffusion index is an attempt to deal with mixed signals from the data. For any collection of series which is meaningful for the forecaster, a diffusion index may be calculated. In a diffusion index 100 indicates that all of the series have risen, zero that all have fallen, and in general the index represents the percentage of the series that have risen during the period of consideration. In computing the percentage of series which have risen, unchanged series are counted as half-rise and half-fall. Interpretation of a diffusion index is perhaps more art than science. A low index number in an expansionary period that is sustained for a number of months should foreshadow a downward turning point (a cyclical peak). A high number in a period of contraction should lead the upturn. How high and how long are largely questions of judgment.

Amplitude-Adjusted Index

The amplitude-adjusted index is a measure of the rate of change of a series or the strength of an expansion. This index too may be computed for any meaningful group of time series and may be a convenient summary statistic for a number of series even if no other use is made of the index.

The procedure is simple. For the group of series being analyzed, the month-to-month percentage change in each series is computed. These new series of percentages are then standardized about a mean equal to one. For each month, compute a weighted average of the standardized values of the various series, using the score assigned to the series as weights. Thus, the highest-scoring series (presumably superior) receives the highest weight. The resulting time series is also standardized about a mean equal to one.

Although this new series is a composite of the several series involved, the index number itself has an interpretation which the forecaster may find useful. If the value of the index for the most recent month is greater than one, the various time series are rising together more rapidly than they have on average in the past. This would be taken to mean that a relatively strong expansion is under way. If, however, the value is less than one, the series are rising less rapidly than they have on average in the past. This would be taken to mean that the expansion is relatively weak or about to reverse.

Of course, the series constructed above could be converted to index numbers and used as such. It is interesting to note that if the series of index numbers so constructed is scored, the score is higher than that of any individual series used to construct the index numbers.

REFERENCES

BUTLER, WILLIAM F. and ROBERT A. KAVESH (eds.). *How Business Economists Forecast.* Englewood Cliffs, N.J.: Prentice-Hall, Inc., 1966.

MOORE, GEOFFREY H. (ed.). *Business Cycle Indications.* Princeton University Press for National Bureau of Economic Research, 1961.

———, and JULIUS SHISKIN. *Indicators of Business Expansions and Contractions.* New York: National Bureau of Economic Research, 1967.

SHISKIN, JULIUS. *Signals of Recession and Recovery.* Occasional Paper 77. New York: National Bureau of Economic Research, 1961.

chapter
—5—
Opportunistic Forecasting

The term "opportunistic" as applied to forecasting must not be viewed in the pejorative sense. The implication is that the forecaster will not depend on any one source or technique but rather will take his information any way he can get it and analyze it by any convenient method. Presumably, such an approach could be used to prepare any type of forecast. Since the technique is a collection of models, it can only be discussed by example. A macroeconomic forecast has many parts and thus serves as a good example. The discussion below, though it only hits the high points, follows closely the technique used successfully for a long time by John Lewis and described in much greater detail in his book with Robert Turner.[1] This chapter is intended only as a brief description of the approach, and any forecaster would be well advised to consult their excellent discussion before attempting to prepare a forecast using their method. Other books in the references at the end of the chapter follow similar methods.

---

[1] J. P. Lewis and R. C. Turner, *Business Conditions Analysis* (New York: McGraw-Hill, 2d ed., 1967).

The approach to the macro forecast involves a series of forecasts of the various sectors of aggregate demand which are part of most standard Keynesian macroeconomic models. The procedure is necessarily iterative. The forecaster starts with the most readily forecast sectors, such as government expenditures. He then proceeds down the list, leaving the more difficult sectors till last. When all have been forecast, a total is computed. It may then be necessary to go back, perhaps more than once, and adjust various subsector forecasts for consistency.

Government Expenditures

Governmental receipts and expenditures may undergo rapid and substantial changes, as recent experience has shown. Nevertheless, even though forecasting the government sector is not necessarily easy, the forecaster can be more sure of his forecast of this sector than of many of the others.

Federal. Determining the spending intentions of the federal government is fairly easy because the process of determining expenditures is well reported. Nevertheless, the process is somewhat lengthy, since expenditures must be budgeted, proposed, debated, and legislated.

The major event of the expenditure determination process is the transmittal of the budget, which occurs in January prior to the start of the fiscal year in July. The document is published as *The Budget of the United States*. The forecaster is most interested in Volume One, though there are at least two other volumes. Other publications of interest are *The Budget in Brief, The Economic Report of the President,* and the February issue of the *Survey of Current Business*. The latter two contain considerable analysis as well.

The forecaster must translate obligational authority, which may extend over several years, into actual expenditures. It should not be too difficult to get good estimates of expenditures except during war periods. There is a certain amount of inertia inherent in the sheer size of the federal government which makes drastic changes from year to year unlikely. Estimation of expenditure for the current budget year and the first half of the next fiscal year is not difficult.

The publication *Midyear Budget Review* is helpful in this regard. The forecaster may have difficulty keeping track of congressional actions, since legislation is enacted almost every day. In preparing a forecast in the fall for the next calendar year, the midyear budget appearing in late summer gives some indication of what has been done in the Congress. If the Congress has adjourned, the forecaster has a good indication of what has been appropriated.

In the past there was a problem of dealing with several budget concepts. While all versions of the budget are still available, the new budget format eliminates some of the problems. There are still critics, but the Bureau of the Budget[2] claims superiority for the new budget format because:

1. It is now comprehensive, in that the trust funds as well as the usual federal funds are considered.
2. Lending programs are separated from spending programs.
3. Receipts of quasi-business governmental agencies are netted against expenditures *of the agency involved*.
4. More prominence is given to actions requested of the Congress.[3]

Of course, the national-income-accounts basis of this executive budget must still be estimated by the forecaster. If he can wait, an issue of the *Survey of Current Business* will help him out somewhat later in the year.

In a sentence then, the procedure is to take the published es-

---

[2] Now included in the Office of Management and Budget.

[3] U.S. Bureau of the Budget, *The Budget in Brief: Fiscal Year 1969* (Washington: Superintendent of Documents, p. 6).

timates, convert to a national-income-accounts basis for the time period of the forecast, and make any adjustments for deviations from the official estimates which the forecaster feels might arise. Since the largest items of the budget are defense, interest on the debt, and veterans' programs the forecaster may want to give these the greatest attention.

State and Local. One may forecast the expenditures of the multitudinous state and local governments by graphing the expenditures for the past five to ten years and using a ruler to extend the line for the period of the forecast. Some slight adjustments may be needed for foreseen variation in tax receipts, financial market conditions, and voter acceptance of bond issues —although extrapolation will provide quite acceptable forecasts.

Business Fixed Investment

The forecast of this sector was discussed above in the chapter on surveys. Use of the McGraw-Hill and Commerce-SEC surveys, prorated to include farm, nonprofit institutions, and oil-well drilling, will provide the most satisfactory estimate of business fixed investment with the least effort.

Housing

The residential housing sector forecast involves estimates of expenditures on replacements as well as net additions to the housing stock. The factors affecting the forecast may be thought of as physical requirements and financial conditions.

Physical. Determination of need in physical terms sets a range. Needs are usually expressed in housing units, not expenditures. The obvious variables to be considered are demographic. The primary demographic variable is net household formation, which is influenced mostly by the age at which people marry and the percent of adults marrying. However, there may be feedback effects, since a shortage of housing may constrain household formation, not vice versa. Other variables to be considered are the rate of doubling and undoubling (i.e., changes in multiple occupancy) and the number of single or nonfamily households.

Family size may also matter; but, since families are flexible with respect to space, this variable is much less important than the number of families as a predictor of the need for housing construction. Over a short period of time, average family size cannot change very much.

The demographic variables discussed above indicate the likelihood of people wanting new housing, but some housing-market variables matter, too.

The rate of vacancies, if far from "normal," may have a strong influence on building activity. Of course, the analyst must consider where the vacancies are located, how long they have existed, and the quality of the vacant units. Any trends in the ownership of second homes should be noted, though to an extent the vacancy rate interacts with this variable.

Finally, there is a certain amount of replacement demand. Some structures are destroyed by fire, flood, and wind and must be replaced. Others are demolished because of alternative demand, leaving the family to replace the structure somewhere else. The alternative demand usually is from business operations and is aimed at the site rather than the structure.

Financial. Having determined at least a range of needed housing units, we next examine the financial-market conditions to pin down the estimate of housing units to be built. The obvious market variable of income turns out to be of little importance in the short run (though not in the long run), unless income is expected to fluctuate violently from past levels.

The important area is credit, especially the supply of credit.

The analyst should consider the amount of credit available, the required size of down payment, and the size of monthly payments. These estimates must be conditioned by considerations of general credit availability and the lending regulations of government agencies, such as VA and FHA. The demand side of the credit market is less important and more difficult to analyze. The forecaster will want to examine, however, the liquidity of potential home buyers and their willingness to take on more debt.

The above analysis will need to be modified within the framework of price and capacity conditions in the construction industry. Shortages of labor and/or material will restrict construction. The analyst should consider whether there is an established trend in housing prices. It is also necessary to consider the spread between prices of old and new houses. Also, new house prices vis-a-vis rent should be examined.

Preparing the Forecast.   The above discussion, instead of detailing the mechanics of estimating the number of housing units to be built during the time period of the forecast, lists the variables which the forecaster should consider. He then converts his unit forecast to a dollar forecast by multiplying by the average price per unit. He determines the average price by dividing recent housing expenditures by the number of units and adjusting the quotient for inflation, upgrading of housing, or forecast housing-price changes. To the estimate of construction expenditures must be added estimates of expenditures on additions, alterations, and nonhousekeeping units to obtain the final housing forecast. Simple extrapolation is good enough for these additional amounts, though the forecaster may be able to get some data on motel and hotel construction.

Automobiles

There are many projections of production of automotive units coming out of the Detroit corporate offices of the automobile manufacturers. However, these are not of interest to the forecaster, as he wants to forecast sales of cars to the final consumer only. Trucks and cars sold to business and government presumably have been picked up elsewhere. The demand for cars is also a function of expansion or contraction demand and replacement demand modified by credit-market conditions.

Expansion or Contraction Demand.   As with housing there are a number of demographic variables to consider. The analyst should consider the rate of household formation, changes (if any) in the ratio of cars to households, and any changes in the age distribution of the population. The latter variable will affect the number of two-car households and/or the demand for sporty models. Price of cars, expectations of changes in prices of cars, and the elasticity of demand for cars will also have to be examined. Similarly, income and expectations about future income are influential. Movement toward suburbia will lead to more two-car families, while movements toward the city will tend to produce apartment-dwelling, no-car families.

Replacement Demand.   This segment of car sales is difficult to forecast, as replacement is not carefully planned and may be an impulse if not brought on by necessity. The forecaster needs to consider as best he can the impact of models and model changes. He will also want to examine the intensity of sales effort. Finally, he will want to discern Detroit policy with respect to dealer receipts of new cars. If Detroit is pushing cars, the dealer will have to figure out how to get rid of them.

Impact of Financial Conditions.   In the area of automobiles, the causation usually runs from decisions to buy to amount of consumer credit outstanding. Very tight credit restrictions may reduce automobile purchases and the forecaster needs to consider this. In addition, he may be able to ascertain from attitude surveys and other sources, the willingness of consumers to take on additional debt.

Preparing the Forecast.   The preparation is the same as for the housing forecast. Estimates of unit sales are adjusted in light of financial conditions if necessary. Historical price per unit is adjusted for forecast price changes and the unit forecast is converted to a dollar forecast by multiplication. It is then necessary to add in an estimate for sales of parts and accessories, extrapolated from past data.

Inventory Investment

The dollar amount of net inventory investment or disinvestment is small relative to other components of GNP, but it is occasionally highly volatile and therefore worth considering. Some forecasters will separate goods in process from finished goods and raw materials, if they think the ratio of goods in process to output will change. However, this amount is very small and may not be worth considering separately.

The first step is to determine secular relationships between sales or output and inventory levels. The forecaster may want to do this separately for durable and nondurable goods industries, since durables are more volatile than nondurables. The ratios are examined to see if they are relatively high or low compared to previous periods and for the existence of any obvious abnormalities. The forecaster should then look for any direct evidence of a change in the ratio of sales to inventory.

To forecast sales one may simply extrapolate the ratio of sales to GNP, using a preliminary estimate of GNP for the moment. If the forecaster feels that there will be any substantial shifts in the composition of GNP, he may want to work with the sectors individually.

With a preliminary estimate of inventory investment or disinvestment, only a few minor adjustments are needed to complete the forecast. One adjustment would be for any foreseen unusual events, such as a possible steel strike. If the forecaster places any credence in inventory cycles, then he will want to adjust for any increase or decrease due to stage of the cycle. Finally, an estimate, usually an extrapolation, for farm inventory investment must be added in.

Net Foreign Investment

This is a very small item in GNP and could even be ignored or left the same as the previous year. A more satisfying estimate may be obtained by separate projections of exports and imports. Simple extrapolation will serve well here, though from time to time it may be necessary to make some adjustments for substantial shifts in policy or economic events of considerable impact. The difference between projected exports and imports is the forecast of net foreign investment.

Consumption Demand Excluding Automobiles

While some of the survey information might be used here, this relationship is more reliably estimated from past relationships by the regression of consumption expenditures on disposable income. The equation would be

$$C_t = a + bY_{Dt} \qquad (5\text{--}1)$$

The forecaster would then forecast disposable income. There is an easier way, which is nothing more than the relationship of disposable income to GNP. Instead, the forecaster estimates the ratio

$$c = \frac{Y_{Dt}}{GNP_t} \qquad (5\text{--}2)$$

Unless there is a substantial change in tax laws, this ratio may be used to estimate

$$C_t = a + bc\ GNP_t \qquad (5\text{--}3)$$

instead of Equation (5-1). The forecast of GNP is then

$$GNP = G + BFI + H + A + II + NFI + C \quad (5-4)$$

where G = Government expenditures; BFI = Business fixed investment; H = Housing; A = Automobiles; II = Inventory investment; NFI = Net foreign investment; and C = Consumption. Substitution of Equation (5-3) into Equation (5-4) gives:

$$GNP = G + BFI + H + A + II + NFI + a + bc\ GNP \quad (5-5)$$

The solution

$$GNP = \frac{a + G + BFI + H + A + II + NFI}{1 - bc} \quad (5-6)$$

is the forecast of GNP. Of course, if the result is very different from the assumed value used to compute some of the forecasts, the process should be repeated several times, until the value obtained stabilizes.

Final Steps

Before making up the final form of the forecast, it may be wise to use the numbers generated to set up a tentative "nation's economic budget." The nation's economic budget is merely a statement balancing national income and expenditures. *Economic Indicators* regularly publishes a historical record of these accounts in this format. Thus, it is possible to check the forecast further for internal consistency.

It will also be necessary to check the forecast against the capacity of the economy. Capacity is a slippery concept, but some estimate of actual or forecast capacity is needed.[4] If the

---

[4] Yost, R. C., "The Capacity Concept and Economic Forecasting," *Mississippi Valley Journal of Business and Economics,* Vol. 1, February 1968, pp. 16–29.

GNP forecast is excessive or deficient with respect to capacity, will there be action taken, particularly in the policy area, which the forecaster needs to consider?

REFERENCES

BUTLER, WILLIAM A. and ROBERT A. KAVESH (eds.). *How Business Economists Forecast.* Englewood Cliffs, N.J.: Prentice-Hall, Inc., 1966.

DAUTEN, CARL A. and LLOYD M. VALENTINE. *Business Cycles and Forecasting,* 3d ed. Cincinnati: Southwestern Publishing Company, 1969.

LEWIS, JOHN P. and ROBERT C. TURNER. *Business Conditions Analysis.* 2d ed., New York: McGraw-Hill Book Co., 1967.

chapter
—6—
Forecasting with Input-Output
Analysis

Input-output analysis is a descriptive model of an economy. Its central concept is "the idea that there is a fundamental relationship between the volume of the output of an industry and the size of the inputs going into it."[1] Its usefulness rests on an assumption of a relatively stable pattern of these relationships.

Input-output tables are nothing more than another form of national income accounting. Input-output analysis uses the same sectors of final demand but breaks down the production by industry of origin. The importance of input-output analysis is that it allows an analysis of all the transactions among industries in the production of gross national product. These transactions are removed from the national income accounts to avoid double counting, while input-output is designed specifically to utilize the intraindustry and interindustry transac-

---

[1] Leontief, W. W., "Input-Output Economics" *Scientific American.* October 1951.

tions. How it does so will become clear from the discussion below.

The recently published tables for the U.S. contain data for almost 370 industries based on 1963 figures.[2] Understanding such a large mass of data is difficult at best. Therefore, an explanation of the input-output tables is developed below for hypothetical economy consisting of three industries, a consumer sector, and a government. For the reader skilled in matrix algebra, footnotes will be employed to discuss the mathematics of input-output. The essence of input-output can be learned without the mathematics through the numerical example. We will start with the simplified income statements for industries *A, B,* and *C* as shown in Table 6–1 in the form of T-accounts. Column (1) indicates expenses plus profits and column (2) indicates receipts.

The above accounts are drawn to reflect interindustry sales and purchases, in order to highlight all the dependencies which exist. Each firm's expenses and profits account reflects inputs, and the receipts account reflects outputs. In Table 6–2 the firms' accounts are aggregated into the appropriate national income and product account. The interindustry transactions are not shown, as they would involve double counting. Gross national income by distributive shares appears in the cost side of the account as charges against the output. Gross national expenditure by sector appears on the income side. Of course, a balance sheet always balances.

---

[2] *Input-Output Structure of the U.S. Economy: 1963;* Volume 1, *Transactions Data for Detailed Industries;* Volume 2, *Direct Requirements for Detailed Industries;* Volume 3, *Total Requirements for Detailed Industries,* Washington, D.C.: U.S. Government Printing Office, December, 1969. The data are also available on magnetic tape for direct input to a computer. The reader should also see: "Input-Output Structure of the U.S. Economy: 1963," *Survey of Current Business,* Vol. IXL, November, 1969, pp. 16–47. This article contains a general description of the new tables plus a condensed 87 industry table which corresponds to the tables published in 1947 and 1958.

TABLE 6–1

Industry Production Accounts

Industry A

(1)		(2)	
Purchases from Industry A	10	Sales to Industry A	10
Wages	80	Sales to Industry B	20
Depreciation	5	Sales to Industry C	30
Profits	15	Sales to Persons	50
	110		110

Industry B

(1)		(2)	
Purchases from Industry A	20	Sales to Industry C	10
Wages	25	Sales to Persons	25
Depreciation	5	Sales to Government	25
Profits	10		
	60		60

Industry C

(1)		(2)	
Purchases from Industry C	10	Sales to Persons	60
Purchases from Industry A	30	Sales to Industry C	10
Purchases from Industry B	10		
Wages	15		
Profits	5		
	70		70

TABLE 6–2

National Income and Product Account

(1)		(2)	
Wages and Salaries	120	Personal Consumption	
Profits	30	Expenditures	135
Depreciation	10	Government	25
GNP	160		160

The Transaction Table

In Table 6–3 below the data from Table 6–1 are combined into the format of the transactions table of input-output. In this form the interindustry flows are preserved, while the final demand vectors (columns 4 and 5) give the same information as the national income accounts.

Each industry is represented by both a row and a column. The *sales or output* of the industry is read across the *row*. The output of each industry purchased as inputs by other industries is read down the columns. It is possible that an industry will purchase some of its own output as inputs ($e_{11}=10$; industry *A* purchases 10 units of itself). The purchases of output by

TABLE 6–3
Input-Output Flow Table

		(1)	(2)	(3)	(4)	(5) Government	(6)
		A	*B*	*C*	*Persons*	*ment*	*Total*
Intermediate	1. A..........	10	20	30	50		110
	2. B..........			10	25	25	60
	3. C..........			10	60		70
Value Added	4. Wages.......	80	25	15			120
	5. Other.......	20	15	5			40
Total.................		110	60	70	135	25	

ultimate consumers is read down the columns headed "Persons" and "Government." Column 6 is the horizontal total of the gross output of each industry.

Table 6–3 has in simplified form all the features found in any transactions tables. For example, notice rows 4 and 5, which are labeled "Value Added." In Table 6–1 the accounting statements of the firms indicated that some factors of production are purchased directly for use in the production of output. The entry for wages in row 4 is the same as shown in Table 6–1. Row 5 is everything else and is labeled simply "Other." Accounting statements being what they are, it is not surprising that the sum of the purchased inputs (column total) is equal to the total output (row total) for each industry. Value Added is simply the resource cost of processing the purchased inputs plus any profit earned.

Reading across row 2, one can see that industry B sells 10 to industry C, 25 to persons, and 25 to government for a total output of 60. Reading down column 2, one finds that industry B purchases inputs of 20 from industry A, pays wages of 25, and has depreciation and profit of 15 for a total cost of producing output of 60.

For the purposes of this simple example, it makes no difference whether the numbers refer to physical units or dollar values. In the published U.S. tables, it is dollar value which is represented. The first and last pages of the transactions table for the United States are reproduced as Table A1 in the appendix to this chapter. The first 13 and the last 9 industry columns are shown as well as the 6 columns of final demand.

The Output Distribution Table

An output distribution table is not included in the regularly published U.S. input-output tables. However, it may be readily derived. This format might be used by a marketing division to compare the pattern of sales by the industry with the distribution of sales of the firm. It would then be possible to ascertain which markets needed more attention.

One can obtain the output distribution table by dividing the rows of the transactions table by the row totals. If the entries of Table 6–3 are divided by the entries in column 6, Table 6–4 is obtained. Column totals have no significance. For ex-

TABLE 6–4

Output Distribution Table

	(1) A	(2) B	(3) C	(4) Persons	(5) Government	(6) Total
1, A.......	.09	.18	.27	.46		1.00
2. B.... ..			.17	.415	.415	1.00
3. C.......			.14	.86		1.00

ample, in row 2 industry B sells 17 percent of its output to industry C and 41.5 percent each to persons and to government.

The Direct Requirements Table

The direct requirements table gives the inputs from each industry named in the left-hand stub required to produce a dollar of output of the industry named at the top of each column. The rows represent the supplying industries. The columns are the producing industries. For the United States as a whole, this has traditionally been Table 2 of the input-output format[3] and is Volume 2 of the expanded version now available. The direct requirements table for the simple economy used as an example above is shown as Table 6–5.

Each entry in Table 6–5 is easily computed. The entry in Table 6–3 is divided by the column total for all columns except gross outputs (column 6).

This table represents the interdependencies of a modern industrial economy. For example, suppose industry C experienced an increase of $1000 in sales. Reading down the column labeled "C," one notes that the required increase in inputs from industry A is $440, from industry B $140, and from within

---

[3] The first two pages of Table 2 for the U.S. economy are shown as Table A2 in the appendix to this chapter. The direct requirement coefficients were derived from the data in Table 1 and refer to 1963 conditions.

industry C $140. In addition, industry C would require $210 more labor and $70 of other inputs.

Total labor required is somewhat greater, however. Industry A will need $440 × .73 = $321.20 more labor, and industry B needs $140 × .42 = $58.80. Because of the increase of $140 in output above the initial $1000 increase, industry C will need $140 × .21 = $29.40 more labor. Thus, the total impact on the labor sector will be $619.40.

TABLE 6–5

Direct Requirements Table

	(1) A	(2) B	(3) C	(4) Persons	(5) Government
1. A..............	.09	.33	.44	.37	
2. B..............			.14	.19	1.00
3. C..............			.14	.44	
4. Wages..........	.73	.42	.21		
5. Other..........	.18	.25	.07		
Total.......	1.00	1.00	1.00	1.00	1.00

The alert reader will already suspect that the direct requirements table does not deal with all the economy. Thus, the direct requirements as illustrated above understate the true impact. Consider again the production of $1000 of output by industry C. In order to produce $1000 for final demand, industry C must produce $140 ($1000 × .14) for its own use. Total output of the industry is then $1140.

In order to produce $1140 of output, industry C requires inputs from the other industries. From industry A, industry C requires $501.60 ($1140 × .44) of output (input to C). From industry B, industry C requires $159.60 ($1140 × .14).

In order to produce an additional $159.60 of output, industry B must purchase $52.67 ($159.60 × .33) of output from industry A. In order for industry C to produce $1000 of output, industry A is required to produce $501.60 plus $52.67 or $554.27 of output for industries B and C. But since industry A uses some of its own output, it must produce $49.88 ($554.27 × .09) for itself or a total of $604.15 output resulting from the $1000 sales of industry C.

In the simple example, neither industry A nor B purchases inputs from industry C. If either did, even more computations would be required to trace through all of the interactions of even a simple economy. For an economy with 87 or 370 industries, the task would be burdensome without the use of large computers. But a computer is not necessary. A table has already been prepared which traces through the total requirements of all industries.

The Total Requirements Table

The total requirements table shows the indirect as well as the direct requirements of each industry listed in the left-hand stub in order to produce a dollars worth of output of the industry listed at the head of each column. With this table it is possible to calculate the total effect on all industries of a change in final demand facing any one of them. This table appears as Table 3 in the 87-industry designation of the U.S. economy[4] and as Volume 3 of the 370-industry tables. The coresponding table for the example economy is shown as Table 6–6 below.

The numbers displayed in Table 6–6 could be computed in the manner outlined above. All the effects of a change could be traced through and the total effect added up. In fact, it is not done this way. The process involved is that of inverting a matrix. Conceptually, inverting a matrix is the same as taking the number 2 and inverting it to obtain the fraction ½. The

---

[4] As above, the first two pages appear as Table A3 in the appendix to this chapter.

reason for doing this is mathematical and is explained in the footnote below. Thus, one obtains Table 6–6 from Table 6–5 by subtracting Table 6–5 from the identity matrix and inverting the result.

Since the entries in this table represent both the direct and indirect requirements of an industry, it is not surprising that the numbers are larger than in the direct requirements table. The entries on the diagonal must be at least unity, since, even if the industry uses none of its own products, it has to at least produce for final demand. For most industries the diagonal entry is greater than unity, since, in order to produce output for final demand, they must produce for internal use.

The figures in Table 6–6 may be used to illustrate the full impact of all the interactions. If industry C is to produce $1000

TABLE 6–6
Total Requirements Table

	(1) A	(2) B	(3) C
1. A.....................	1.099	.363	.622
2. B.....................		1.000	.163
3. C.....................			1.163

output for final demand, it must produce $1163 in total, slightly more than the $1140 calculated from the direct requirements table. Similarly, when all the interactions are considered, $1000 output of industry C requires $622 output from industry A and $163 output from industry B. The direct requirements alone were calculated at $604.15 and $159.60, respectively.[5]

---

[5] For the mathematically skilled reader, the last several paragraphs may be summarized as follows. The input-output model is

$$X = AX + D \qquad (1)$$

where X is the vector of total outputs (column 6 of Table 6–3), A is

Using the Input-Output Tables

In order to use the input-output tables, the forecaster needs to be aware of some of the underlying assumptions and definitions employed in the construction of the tables. Further, one must carry out a number of conversions of current or forecast data before using the technique to prepare any kind of a forecast. Each of these factors will be discussed in turn.

Assumptions and Definitions. In the construction of the basic transactions table, the following definitions are used. Gross output of an industry is defined as the total production of both primary and secondary products and services of the industry plus the producers' value of the secondary products or services of other industries which are primary to the industry in question plus the domestic port value of substitutable imports which are distributed to final users as output of the given industry. Gross inputs are defined as the total usage in dollar terms of all goods and services purchased for production of output plus the value added by the industry plus the producers' value of secondary products and services of other industries which are primary to the given industry plus the domestic port value of substitutable imports. Several additional comments are required for clarification of above statements.

In the current U.S. tables the data are all collected in terms of producers' prices as of 1963. The user of the tables must be

---

Table 6–5, and D is final demand (columns 4 and 5 of Table 6–3).
Solving Equation (1) for D gives

$$D = (I - A)X \tag{2}$$

where I is the identity matrix.
Solving (2) for X gives

$$X = (I - A)^{-1}D$$

$(I - A)^{-1}$ is the total requirements table (Table 6–6). The $^{-1}$ notation refers to the inverse of the $(I - A)$ matrix as explained in the text above.

willing to assume that prices have not changed, or he must be able to convert his data to the 1963 levels. Producers' prices exclude distribution costs. The trade (industry 69) and transportation (industry 65) industries provide the distribution services. These services are separated out of any transaction, whether it be between two industries or between an industry and a final consumer. The *goods* are *valued* at producers' prices, while the trade or transportation services are given separately as an input to the consuming industry or the final user.

Most firms and industries are difficult to classify because they produce a variety of products. Firms are classified by the industry in which their most important or primary product belongs. The secondary products are also treated as part of the output of the industry of which the firm is a part. But this output of secondary products is treated as if it were sold to the industry for which it is a primary product, regardless of where the output is actually sold. Then, the sale of all the products to the ultimate purchaser is recorded as an output of the industry for which the products are primary even though they were not actually produced by firms of that industry.

Similarly, imports which are substitutable for domestic products are added as inputs and outputs of the industry producing that commodity. If the import is different from any domestic product, it is added only as a purchase of the consuming industry of final user. Changes in the pattern of secondary product production or of importing will obviously change the data of the input-output table.

The industries are classified into 85 industries of the usual sort and three distribution industries in the smaller tables. In the larger tables the above categories are broken down into from one to thirty-two smaller industry groupings for the total of nearly 370.[6] The categories in the larger table are roughly

---

[6] See *Survey of Current Business,* November, 1969, pp. 26–29.

similar to a four-digit Standard Industrial Classification (SIC) code industry, though some of the input-output categories are more aggregative. Implicit in any aggregation of industries are a number of assumptions. If the input-output coefficients are meaningful, it is assumed implicitly that the coefficient holds for all firms and/or industries in the grouping, that all the firms/industries vary their output in step with each other as final demand changes, and that there is a stability in the product mix of each sector.

The additional assumption that the underlying production processes may be described by a linear homogeneous production function has a number of implications. Use of a linear, homogeneous production function means that for constant factor prices there will be no substitution between the various inputs and that changes in output will be in proportion to changes in the level of the constant input mix. Further, the user must be willing to assume that the implied coefficients of the production function, as determined in the input-output table, have not changed over time because of technological change or for any other reason. This is a heroic assumption, since the most recent data base is 1963.

It is also assumed that the calendar year is the relevant time period for the production process. Whether it is or not is less important than the willingness on the part of the forecaster to assume that the average time period of the production process has not changed since 1963. Also, when time enters the production process, changes in inventories must be considered. In the U.S. tables the figure for inventory change relates to the products of the industry regardless of which industry is currently holding those inventories.

Procedures. In order to use input-output, the forecaster must follow a number of supplementary procedures. Of course, if all he is concerned with is forecasting industry requirements from a forecast of industry output, these procedures involve only correcting for price change. Use of the Consumer Price Index, the Wholesale Price Index, or the GNP deflator, whichever is appropriate, is all that is required. Full information on the price adjustments is at this writing still forthcoming from the Office of Business Economics.

A more common situation is one in which the forecaster will have a projection of final demand, either in total or broken down in some way. From this final demand forecast, a bill of goods must be prepared. The bill of goods is nothing more than the final demand segmented into demands for each industry expressed in 1963 producers' prices. For this bill of goods the required trade and transportation services will also have to be estimated as output of these industries. The data required to make the conversions indicated are available in the article in the November, 1969, *Survey of Current Business* which contains the input-output tables.

Additional Input-Output Tables

Other sources in addition to the government prepare input-output tables, though the basis for the private tables is frequently the government tables. The purpose of the private efforts has been to update and expand the existing tables. Since another purpose of the private efforts has been to make a profit, the tables or forecasts prepared from them may be expensive.

For a modest charge *Scientific American* offers a chart based on 1966 levels of GNP. In addition, the user may borrow a movie explaining the process of input-output analysis.

One of the updated and expanded versions is offered by IBM and Dun & Bradstreet. The table is expanded to the 4-digit SIC level and has about 250 rows and 500 columns. There are additional marketing services offered as well.

Another private source is *Fortune* working with CEIR, Inc. Their offering is on a 1966 base and is expanded to 106 industries. Those wishing greater detail may disaggregate to the 7-digit SIC level of classification.

Some firms have prepared their own input-output tables. One firm has a table of 90 industries heavily representing their customers. Another firm has a 120-industry model which was in use as early as 1963.

Uses of Input-Output in Forecasting

The following discussion is divided into two parts. The first describes the macro uses, which usually refer to forecasts at the level of the federal government, though regional and statewide tables are also available. The micro uses are at the level of the firm. The tables may be used in the several ways listed below, or forecasts at the firm level may be produced by employing the modification of the tables suggested.

Macroeconomic Forecasts. A study has been published in which input-output techniques form the basis of a forecast of the U.S. economy to 1975.[7] The model forecasts a 3.8 percent overall growth rate with sector rates from as high as 6.3 percent for rubber and plastics to an actual decline of −0.1 percent for "other transportation equipment." The only operational assumptions are that the unemployment rate will average under 4 percent for the entire period and that there will be a post-Vietnam period starting after the 1968 elections. Since this happy event had not yet occurred by mid-1971, the estimates are likely in error.

Further development and continued usage of the model are contemplated. Perhaps other considerations, such as price-level changes, may be forecast. Before this may be done, additional work must be done on the linkage equations which translate

---

[7] Almon, C., Jr., *The American Economy to 1975*. New York: Harper & Row, 1967. For a short summary, see "What Input-Output Tells Industry," *Business Week*, December 9, 1967, pp. 88–95.

the level of output in one period into the final demand vectors for the next period. The consumption equations predict expenditures for 79 broad segments of consumer *spending* based on income levels and the relative price-level changes between sectors. There are also capital goods equations for 69 industries. Additional empirical studies and expert opinion will be sought to improve these equations and perhaps introduce variable input-output coefficients into the model. The model is in use by the forecasting group at the University of Maryland, and the forecasts prepared appear in the press from time to time, particularly in the *Wall Street Journal* and *Business Week*.

Government predictions of long-term economic growth have also been prepared. The implications of growth for manpower requirements have been studied as well as the impact on various industries and/or regions of changing export or import markets or the location of a highway or other construction. States have used input-output to study alternative courses of economic development or alternative tax programs, especially where it is expected that the particular policies will have differential industrial impact. States have also fed economic and demographic forecasts into input-output systems to plan land use, highway construction, expenditure and revenue programs, and industrial development. Input-output has been used in many areas to forecast water needs in urban areas, by industry, or for irrigation or recreational uses.

Microeconomic Forecasts.   The main use at the micro level is forecasting sales potential of a given firm. The tables allow a formal analysis of the implications of changes in final demand for the sales of an industry and the firm which is a member of that industry.

Besides analyzing sales potential for the industry, the firm may also forecast requirements for inputs, making sure it has sufficient sources of supply. Further, because of the tendency of industries to be distributed in uneven geographic patterns, input-output may be used to analyze changing market patterns and solve problems of plant and warehouse location. Input-output has been used to analyze potential sales of new products as well as to forecast changes in sales of existing products.

Consider the following simple example—overly simple since it is impossible on the pages of a book to appeal to a computer. In the U.S. tables, industry 13 is called ordnance and accessories. According to Table 1 of the U.S. tables, industry 13 purchased $193 million at producers' prices from industry 38, Primary Nonferrous Metal Manufacturing.[8] Industry 38 is the third largest supplying industry of industry 13, though industry 13 takes only a little more than 1 percent of the output of industry 38. (The reader should verify these statements in Table A1 of the U.S. tables in the appendix to this chapter.)

Copper is a nonferrous metal. Suppose a copper smelting firm is interested in the impact on industry sales of an expected $10 million reduction of purchases of ordnance. One could forecast the direct effect by consulting Table 2 of the U.S. tables; the appropriate coefficient is 0.03066.[9] Thus, the direct decline in sales of industry 38 is $306,600.

Of course, the total impact on sales of industry 38 will depend on tracing through all of the effects of the reduction in sales by industry 13. The total impact on industry 38 may be forecast by the appropriate coefficient from Table 3 of the U.S. tables.[10] The coefficient is 0.09180, and the total decline in sales of industry 38 is $918,000.

There are many nonferrous metals important to ordnance. Lead is the first to come to mind, but a moment's reflection leads one to think of aluminum and zinc as well. The copper-producing firm may well feel that it would like more detailed forecasts. The 370-industry tables allow such a forecast. A por-

---

[8] *Survey of Current Business,* November, 1969, p. 30.

[9] *Ibid.,* p. 37., and in Table A2 in the appendix below.

[10] *Ibid.,* p. 43., and in Table A3 in the appendix below.

tion of Volume 3 of the larger U.S. tables is reproduced below in Table 6–7.

Even this small portion of the enlarged tables reveals the value of being able to separate the effect on a particular subset of an "industry" of the 87-sector table. Suppose, for example, that the copper producer mentioned above knows that his only customer in ordnance is a producer of fire control equipment and, further, that of the $10 million cut in ordnance expenditures only $1 million will be cut from the budget for this type of equipment.

The supplying firm is in industry 38.01, and the purchaser is in industry 13.04. The coefficient is .00842, so the reduction in sales of primary copper is $8,420. Since the firm has only a portion of the total sales of industry 38.01, some allocation of this reduction must be made.

Another way has been suggested by which the firm might modify existing input-output tables to make them useful for forecasting directly at the firm level rather than having to work with market shares of industry output. This alternative allows the firm to disaggregate the tables to the level of the firm with due consideration of the product mix of the firm rather than the pattern of the industry.[11]

While the suggested approach necessarily requires certain assumptions to be made, it has the advantage of being simple enough to work out on a desk calculator. In essence, the approach is restricted to the output side, since unless a firm is quite large one may ignore the impact of its purchases and thus not bother to insert a column.

The firm starts by having the marketing department estimate the firm's sales, in either dollar or percentage terms, to each of the sectors in the table. To calculate its row in the

---

[11] Tiebout, C. M., "Input-Output and the Firm. A Technique for Using National and Regional Tables," *Review of Economics and Statistics*. V. 49, 1966, pp. 260–62.

TABLE 6-7

Portion of Total Requirements Table for U.S. Economy

	Industry 13—Ordnance and Accessories						
	13.01 Complete guided missiles	13.02 Ammunition, except for small arms	13.03 Tanks and tank components	13.04 Sighting and fire control equipment	13.05 Small arms	13.06 Small arms ammunition	13.07 Other ordnance and accessories
Industry 38—Primary Nonferrous Metals Manufacturing:							
38.01 Primary copper	.00430	.01144	.01204	.00842	.00447	.07651	.00811
38.02 Primary lead	.00095	.00147	.00271	.00096	.00264	.08400	.00140
38.03 Primary zinc	.00100	.00174	.00256	.00180	.00105	.00956	.00133
38.04 Primary aluminum	.00126	.03877	.05707	.01035	.00158	.01265	.01847
38.05 Primary nonferrous metals	.00329	.00503	.00836	.00307	.00334	.00482	.00447
38.06 Secondary nonferrous metals	.00306	.00797	.01149	.00339	.00289	.04666	.00487
38.07 Copper rolling and drawing	.00420	.01491	.01089	.00431	.00603	.13852	.00617
38.08 Aluminum rolling and drawing	.01379	.06658	.09096	.00542	.00637	.01432	.01307
38.09 Nonferrous rolling and drawing	.00729	.00449	.00529	.00321	.00249	.00129	.00816
38.10 Nonferrous wire drawing and insulating	.00361	.00536	.00658	.00466	.00114	.00767	.00289
38.11 Aluminum castings	.00330	.00257	.01703	.02120	.00313	.00035	.00399
38.12 Brass, bronze, and copper castings	.00127	.00162	.00346	.01598	.00052	.00038	.00961
38.13 Nonferrous castings	.00080	.00087	.00276	.00520	.00042	.00011	.00101
38.14 Nonferrous forgings	.00836	.00666	.01955	.00021	.00979	.00021	.01198

Source: *Input-Output Structure of the U.S. Economy: 1963*; Volume 3, "Total Requirements for Detailed Industries," pp. 13, 18.

transactions table, the firm needs only divide the dollar sales to any industry in the table by the total inputs purchased by that industry. This is the a_{ij} entry for that firm selling to each industry (the A matrix of footnote 5).

One may calculate an output distribution table using the a_{ij}'s and the percentage distributions of sales. Thus, the firm may know how much of its output is tied directly and indirectly through sales to other industries to any sector of final demand.

The entry in the total requirements table may also be determined. This is the $(I - A)^{-1}$ matrix. In matrix notation, what is desired is the $a_{ij}\,(I - A)^{-1}$ vector, which can be interpreted as another row of the former $(I - A)^{-1}$ matrix.

An example using the U.S. tables will help. To calculate the entry in, say, column 11, new construction, the forecaster would start down that column. In row 1, livestock and livestock products, is the entry 0.0048. This is the increase in output of industry 1, transmitted through industry 11, resulting from an increase in final demand. The a_{ij} which reflects the firm's sales to industry 1 multiplied by .0048 gives the impact on the firm transmitted through livestock and livestock products.

The forecaster repeats the process for each entry in column 11, using the appropriate a_{ij} for the firm. Since some of the entries or some of the a_{ij}'s may be zero, there will not be 87 non-zero products. However, the sum of the products obtained becomes a new entry, perhaps row 88 in column 11.

Completion of the same procedure for each of the other 86 columns will result in a new row 88 of the $(I - A)^{-1}$ matrix. (Volume 3 of the published version, Table 6–6 in the example above.) The forecaster is now ready to forecast the change in demand for his firm's products for a change in final demand of any of the 87 industries.

PROBLEMS

1. Using Table A1 of the 87 industry tables, identify those industries which sold all of their output to final demand; three fourths or more to final demand.

2. Assume a $1 million increase in sales of automobiles. What would be the direct and indirect effects on sales of:

steel	limestone	synthetic fibers
chemicals	coal	electricity
iron ore	natural fibers	containers

REFERENCES

BAHL, R. W., and K. L. SHELLHAMMER. "Evaluating the State Business Tax Structure: An Application of Input-Output Analysis." *National Tax Journal,* Vol. XXII, June, 1969, pp. 203–16.

BRADLEY, I. E., and J. P. GANDER. "Utah Interindustry Study: An Application of Input-Output Analysis." *Utah Economics and Business Review,* Vol. XVIII, February, 1968, pp. 1–13.

HARMISTON, F. K., and R. E. LUND. *Application of an Input-Output Framework to a Community Economic System.* Columbia, Mo.: University of Missouri Press, 1967.

HAVEMAN, ROBERT H., and JOHN V. KRUTILLA. *Unemployment, Idle Capacity, and the Evaluation of Public Expenditures: National and Regional Analysis.* Baltimore: John Hopkins Press, 1968.

JENSEN, B. C. *The Impact of Reparations on the Post-War Finnish Economy: An Input-Output Study.* Homewood, Ill.: Richard D. Irwin, Inc., 1966.

MATHUR, P. N., and R. BHARADWAJ (eds.). *Economic Analysis in Input-Output Framework.* Poona, India: Input-Output Research Association, 1968.

MIERNYK, W. H. "Long-Range Forecasting with a Regional Input-Output Model." *Western Economics Journal,* Vol. VI, June, 1968.

————. *The Elements of Input-Output Analysis*. New York: Random House, 1965.

PATERSON, R. W. *Forecasting Techniques for Determining the Potential Demands for Highways*. Columbia, Mo.: Business and Public Administration Research Center, University of Missouri, 1966.

PETERSON, I. D. *Economic Structure of Idaho — A Provisional Input-Output Study*. Idaho BBER Research Report No. 12. Moscow: Bureau of Business and Economic Research, College of Business Administration, University of Idaho, 1968.

TIEBOUT, C. M. "An Empirical Regional Input-Output Projection Model: The State of Washington, 1980." *Review of Economics and Statistics,* Vol. LI, August, 1969.

UDIS, B. "Regional Input-Output Analysis and Water Quality Management" *Rocky Mountain Social Sciences Journal.*

Use of Input-Output Analysis as an Aid in Forecasting in the Capital Goods Industries. New York: Machinery and Allied Products Institute.

YAN, C. S. *Introduction to Input-Output Economics*. New York: Holt, Rinehart and Winston, 1968.

APPENDIX TO CHAPTER 6

The following pages contain portions of the condensed U.S. tables from the November, 1969, issue of *Survey of Current Business*. Table A1 of the appendix is the first and last pages of Table 1, the interindustry transfer table for 1963. The direct and total requirements tables, Tables 2 and 3, are also partially reproduced as Table A2 and Table A3. For the complete tables the reader should see the above-mentioned issue of the *Survey of Current Business*.

TABLE A1 Interindustry Transactions, 1963

[In millions of dollars at producers' prices]

For the distribution of output of an industry, read the row for that industry.

For the composition of inputs to an industry, read the column for that industry.

Industry No.	Industry	1. Livestock and live-stock products	2. Other agricultural products	3. Forestry and fishery products	4. Agricultural, forestry and fishery services	5. Iron and ferroalloy ores mining	6. Nonferrous metal ores mining	7. Coal mining	8. Crude petroleum and natural gas	9. Stone and clay mining and quarrying	10. Chemical and fertil-izer mineral mining	11. New construction	12. Maintenance and repair construction	13. Ordnance and accessories
1	Livestock & Livestock Products	4,750	1,819	117	192							323	(*)	(*)
2	Other Agricultural Products	7,897	769	117	550							3	(*)	(*)
3	Forestry & Fishery Products	445	1,053	35										
4	Agricultural, Forestry & Fishery Services			74										1
5	Iron & Ferroalloy Ores Mining					55	1							
6	Nonferrous Metal Ores Mining	6	1			25	283			5	1			
7	Coal Mining					5	1	410		5	1	478	259	
8	Crude Petroleum & Natural Gas	1	85				6	1	297			17	7	6
9	Stone and Clay Mining and Quarrying		35			5		14	379	17	31	5	3	161
10	Chemical & Fertilizer Mineral Mining	200	367	44	34	1	7			1		26		
11	New Construction		2							11	3			
12	Maintenance & Repair Construction								2			31		
13	Ordnance & Accessories	3,554			41							124	13	4
14	Food & Kindred Products								2			29		
15	Tobacco Manufactures		2									7	3	
16	Broad & Narrow Fabrics, Yarn & Thread Mills	9	9	62		2	10	17		(*)	20	3,553	723	16
17	Miscellaneous Textile Goods & Floor Coverings	9	29	1	14							7		5
18	Apparel	17	43							6		342	71	2
19	Miscellaneous Fabricated Textile Products	2	2									184		3
20	Lumber & Wood Products, Except Containers		97									208	54	7
21	Wooden Containers											4		1
22	Household Furniture	12			86									2
23	Other Furniture & Fixtures	3	1	(*)	1					(*)		201		3
24	Paper & Allied Products, Except Containers	5	3	(*)		21	56	38	101	34	20	1	54	7
25	Paperboard Containers & Boxes	57		2								2		1
26	Printing & Publishing		9		3							201		16
27	Chemicals & Selected Chemical Products	83	1,424	(*)	(*)	11	7	23	64	52	6	308	869	1
28	Plastics & Synthetic Materials					7	10	33	16	70		1,119	540	13
29	Drugs, Cleaning & Toilet Preparations	170	954	4	3							487	139	103
30	Paints & Allied Products	29	114	34	(*)							1		(*)
31	Petroleum Refining & Related Industries			1						116		81	93	
32	Rubber & Miscellaneous Plastics Products	7			3	4	2	3	41	28	14	5,813	410	149
33	Leather Tanning & Industrial Leather Products	5				21	27	39	30	1	2	2,125	317	193
34	Footwear & Other Leather Products	1	39			1	(*)					1,244	209	
35	Glass & Glass Products													
36	Stone & Clay Products													
37	Primary Iron & Steel Manufacturing	1	1											
38	Primary Nonferrous Metal Manufacturing	8	13											
39	Metal Containers			21										

40 Heating, Plumbing & Structural Metal Products	25				(*)	2	12	18	2	1		6,159	569	10
41 Stampings, Screw Machine Products & Bolts	21											975	112	35
42 Other Fabricated Metal Products	31	31	15	132	1	4	36	13	4	1	2	269	35
43 Engines & Turbines					8	11	85	16	37	5		3
44 Farm Machinery & Equipment	5				24	30	1		48	16	238	26	(*)
45 Construction, Mining & Oil Field Machinery	229	229		26	24	3	5	25	16	4	257	71	3
46 Materials Handling Machinery & Equipment					(*)	1					11	96	1
47 Metalworking Machinery & Equipment					1							(*)	22
48 Special Industry Machinery & Equipment	3												
49 General Industrial Machinery & Equipment		7				1	2	25	23	2	210	43	20
50 Machine Shop Products	7	7				1	11	(*)	8	2	12	1	13
51 Office, Computing & Accounting Machines						32							
52 Service Industry Machines										5	404	116	10
53 Electric Industrial Equipment & Apparatus					(*)	1	7	82	7	5	337	56	25
54 Household Appliances	1	1									184	99	5
55 Electric Lighting & Wiring Equipment			36			1	11		1	1	1,123	183	46
56 Radio, Television & Communication Equipment								4			79	20	281
57 Electronic Components & Accessories			(*)					15	1	(*)	1	1	106
58 Miscellaneous Electrical Machinery, Equipment & Supplies	6	25				2	8	1	15		37	10	18
59 Motor Vehicles & Equipment	7	14	2		2			3			36	14	1
60 Aircraft & Parts													1,868
61 Other Transportation Equipment	(*)	4	21			2	9	4	(*)		4	(*)	17
62 Scientific & Controlling Instruments	4		1			1					208	70	40
63 Optical, Ophthalmic & Photographic Equipment	2	2										(*)	53
64 Miscellaneous Manufacturing	308	308	44	26	126	30	46	281	34	39	89	77	1
65 Transportation & Warehousing	606	83			2	2	4	9	1	3	2,143	490	28
66 Communications; Except Radio & TV Broadcasting	52										180	79	52
67 Radio & TV Broadcasting													
68 Electric, Gas, Water & Sanitary Services	96	204	(*)	1	27	41	65	141	62	36	205	90	26
69 Wholesale & Retail Trade	870	843	56	42	21	28	58	145	54	14	5,453	1,702	93
70 Finance & Insurance	156	315	3	6	7	25	28	94	29	6	401	161	27
71 Real Estate & Rental	289	2,020		41	111	42	73	2,246	45	11	307	134	30
72 Hotels; Personal & Repair Services exc. Auto			1										10
73 Business Services	139	836	7	(*)	33	14	28	108	22	6	2,959	281	110
75 Automobile Repair & Services	76	161		1	1	2	8	42	19	1	235	101	9
76 Amusements	181												
77 Medical, Educational Services & Nonprofit Organizations	(*) 4	13			1	1	2	5	2	2	57	24	8
78 Federal Government Enterprises	1	4	(*)		1	1	2	5	2	2	18	8	10
79 State & Local Government Enterprises	214	1	(*)		1	1	1	3	1	1	28	10	(*)
80A Directly Allocated Imports	2												
80B Transferred Imports	174												
81 Business Travel, Entertainment & Gifts	174	221	428		423	213	2	1,046	108	88	359	154	18
82 Office Supplies	18	32	18		3	(*)	11	67	11	(*)	17	7	49
83 Scrap, Used & Secondhand Goods	1	1	(*) 5	16	(*) 1	5	1	5	1	1	38		10
84 Government Industry							1						
85 Rest of the World Industry													
86 Household Industry													
87 Inventory Valuation Adjustment													
I. Intermediate Inputs, Total	19,992	12,437	1,153	1,190	954	893	1,097	5,338	901	336	39,629	8,663	3,777
V.A. Value Added	6,692	14,830	598	582	475	625	1,540	6,926	1,123	360	25,890	11,132	2,525
T. Total	26,684	27,266	1,751	1,772	1,429	1,519	2,637	12,265	2,024	696	65,519	19,794	6,302
TR. Transfers 1	210	261	709	650	555	237	3	1,865	268	116			1,589

*Less than $500,000.

1. Entry in each column represents the sum of the value of transferred imports at domestic port value and the value of the secondary output of other industries which has been transferred to the industry named at the head of the column. See text for further discussion.

2. The detailed entries reflect gross exports of goods and services from each producing industry. Imports in total are shown as negative entries in this column on rows 80A and 80B. Therefore, the sum of the column equals the GNP component "net exports of goods and services."

Source: *Survey of Current Business*, November, 1969, pp. 30 and 35.

TABLE A1—Continued

[In millions of dollars at producers' prices]

Note: The table is printed sideways (rotated 90°) on the page. Columns 80A & 80B (Gross imports of goods and services), 84 (Government industry), 85 (Rest of the world industry), 86 (Household industry) and 87 (Inventory valuation adjustment) contain no entries for these rows and are shown as dashes. A "(*)" in the source denotes a value less than rounding; "—" denotes a blank (dotted) cell.

Industry No.	Transfers [3]	Total	Total final demand	State and local government purchases	Federal Government purchases	Net exports [2]	Net inventory change	Gross private fixed capital formation	Personal consumption expenditures	Intermediate outputs, total	83 Scrap, used and second-hand goods	82 Office supplies	81 Business travel, entertainment and gifts	79 State and local government enterprises
1	2,026	26,684	2,193	12	5	38	374	—	1,762	24,492	—	—	36	2
2	2,681	27,266	6,365	88	-92	2,917	584	—	2,868	20,901	—	—	107	(*)
3	7	1,751	340	2	-172	46	44	—	420	1,411	—	—	7	1
4	7	1,772	9	-33	17	11	-55	—	15	1,762	—	—	—	81
5	14	1,429	72	—	9	118	-3	—	165	1,357	—	—	—	39
6	40	1,519	239	14	242	305	(*)	—	—	1,279	—	—	—	2
7	16	1,637	520	-30	35	12	16	—	15	12,237	9	(*)	—	1,307
8	622	2,285	27	24	(*)	38	1	—	2,069	1,998	92	—	8	(*)
9	87	2,024	26	—	—	62	-1	—	166	1,541	—	—	3	1
10	217	696	88	—	3	2	—	5	2	609	3	—	—	2
11	—	65,519	65,519	15,356	4,010	197	-26	46,151	181	14,871	—	—	—	(*)
12	454	19,794	4,924	3,510	1,414	1,648	583	—	49,921	648	—	—	—	—
13	3,099	6,302	5,654	2	5,300	508	23	—	4,943	21,306	—	—	—	—
14	187	74,263	52,957	488	317	281	33	—	630	1,950	—	—	8	1,307
15	832	13,131	5,474	1	33	29	83	63	1,011	12,141	—	—	—	—
16	210	3,668	990	14	12	147	67	—	13,697	3,974	—	(*)	—	—
17	264	18,029	14,055	(*)	69	35	40	5	13,482	1,541	—	—	—	(*)
18	160	3,174	1,634	75	69	194	63	—	230	10,152	—	—	3	2
19	229	10,654	1,502	8	6	2	1	—	3,025	412	8	—	—	(*)
20	34	420	7	3	4	10	73	124	133	800	92	—	—	—
21	142	4,067	3,267	7	17	19	14	1,127	1,241	382	8	—	4	22
22	103	1,923	1,540	18	42	449	90	—	74	11,248	3	421	10	—
23	841	13,119	1,872	205	47	23	33	—	394	4,550	—	1,208	1	(*)
24	159	13,748	199	45	10	163	109	—	3,160	12,285	23	10	52	2
25	8,406	16,283	3,999	59	117	1,160	88	—	14,009	5,708	36	—	—	(*)
26	1,303	16,893	2,885	450	1,036	553	25	—	12	2,702	78	—	—	—
27	649	6,341	633	206	42	335	160	—	5,428	2,363	—	—	3	—
28	147	9,053	6,351	(*)	73	31	39	—	23	11,737	—	—	30	55
29	—	2,462	—	355	3	678	177	18	8,232	7,357	10	10	3	7
30	1,651	21,837	10,100	301	711	276	105	—	1,863	933	12	—	2	(*)
31	696	9,891	2,534	101	171	41	-8	—	3,032	420	8	(*)	—	19
32	23	967	34	—	4	18	-48	—	238	2,484	1	—	—	12
33	113	3,427	3,007	1	12	96	68	—	217	9,097	—	—	—	—
34	61	2,932	448	33	23	128	71	—	10	23,965	—	—	—	—
35	556	9,548	450	13	45	493	102	—	—	—	—	—	—	—
36	1,526	24,618	653	3	—	—	—	—	—	—	135	4	—	—

	(1)	(2)	(3)	(4)	(5)	(6)	(7)	(8)	(9)	(10)
38	886	14,272	636	{ }	-11	491	122	22	12	13,635
39	86	2,445	68	11	7	25	28	9	88	2,377
40	627	8,996	1,021	8	58	252	86	536	266	7,975
41	559	4,955	405	15	28	44	56	242	580	4,551
42	713	8,963	1,222	33	40	289	93	388	125	7,742
43	295	3,080	1,022	1	179	303	27	1,902	10	1,376
44	341	4,062	2,270	22	11	285	46	1,760		810
45	407	1,617	2,887	7	105	936	52	665	77	1,175
46	180	5,144	844	12	70	96	12	2,025	21	773
47	384	3,716	2,334	43	86	423	56	1,386		2,810
48	421	5,354	2,656		17	561	25		2	1,061
49	608	2,257	2,055		236	378	43			3,299
50	194		109		49		9	6		2,148
51	543	3,925	2,619	111	448	317	41	1,615	88	1,305
52	363	3,391	1,828	73	47	209	52	1,112	336	1,563
53	739	6,495	2,733	61	423	343	23	1,862	22	3,762
54	848	4,673	3,280	14	10	132	211	120	2,793	1,303
55	301	3,081	653	54	13	81	27	55	422	2,428
56	1,201	12,440	9,332	116	4,686	366	151	1,924	2,089	3,108
57	379	4,512	865	5	398	199	-9	98	176	3,647
58	275	2,256	793	13	110	75	28	198	368	1,464
59	1,230	40,031	24,357	644	663	1,386	611	5,671	15,381	15,674
60	2,019	14,317	9,226	(*)	7,532	857	342	446	49	5,091
61	372	4,290	3,811	30	1,124	165	46	1,465	980	1,084
62	603	2,534	2,028	118	405	373	58	673	403	2,252
63	385	7,152	1,327	65	147	157	14	340	3,327	1,207
64	1,084	39,215	4,170	102	8	186	49	497	8,946	2,983
65	4,493	13,495	14,715	682	1,320	3,040	152	574	5,542	24,500
66	553		6,755	344	341	43		485		6,740
67	2,234	2,308	44	17		28			11,358	2,264
68	132	29,660	12,513	860	264	30		4,858	80,791	17,148
69		120,613	88,551	114	728	1,735	325	1	16,879	32,063
70	1,124	33,700	17,222	268	37	37		1,224	53,878	16,478
71	14	83,887	56,140	478	162	397			12,074	27,747
72	1,414	15,370	12,603	163	361	4			2,967	2,767
73	672	35,945	6,108	962	1,981	199			6,693	29,837
74	96	10,866	6,813	99	21		6		4,712	4,054
75	403	7,697	5,085	-53	107	313			29,335	2,612
76	112	5,864	31,506	723	1,416	32			888	1,654
77	1,214	7,236	1,276	182	115	90			638	4,588
78	6,011		858	21	198		21	166	6,064	6,378
79			-3,477	3	2,649	-12,320				3,477
80A			-14,318			-14,318				14,318
80B	14,318									
81		7,793	385	243	143	329	106		-250	
82		2,106	-334	506	-53					
83		1,518		30,581	24,449	6,208		-972	-1,382	
84		55,029	55,029		-643				3,824	
85		4,183	4,183							
86		502	502							
87										
V.A.										
T.										
T.R.		590,389	590,389	59,082	64,115	5,812	5,329	80,510	375,540	

Source: *Survey of Current Business*, November, 1969, pp. 36-37.

TABLE A2 Direct Requirements per Dollar of Gross Output, 1963

[Producers' prices]

For the composition of inputs to an industry, read the column for that industry.

Column key:
1. Livestock and livestock products
2. Other agricultural products
3. Forestry and fishery products
4. Agricultural, forestry and fishery services
5. Iron and ferroalloy ores mining
6. Nonferrous metal ores mining
7. Coal mining
8. Crude petroleum and natural gas
9. Stone and clay mining and quarrying
10. Chemical and fertilizer mineral mining
11. New construction

Industry No.	Industry	1	2	3	4	5	6	7	8	9	10	11
1	Livestock & Livestock Products	0.17800	0.06673	0.06687	0.10823							0.00493
2	Other Agricultural Products	.29596	.02319	.06665	.31040							.00005
3	Forestry & Fishery Products	.01667	.03863	.01992	.01933							
4	Agricultural, Forestry & Fishery Services			.04243								.00215
5	Iron & Ferroalloy Ores Mining					0.03846	0.00089	0.00004		0.00002		
6	Nonferrous Metal Ores Mining	.00021	.00002			.01782	.17332	.00010	0.00002	.00225	0.00013	
7	Coal Mining					.00361	.00090	.15561	(*)	.00227	.00087	
8	Crude Petroleum & Natural Gas	.00006	.00311			.00339	.00029	.00026	.02418	.00860	.00772	.00729
9	Stone and Clay Mining and Quarrying		.00129				.00408	.00001		.00072	.04442	
10	Chemical & Fertilizer Mineral Mining											
11	New Construction	.00750	.01344			.00060	.00491	.00549	.03093	.00543	.00394	.00027
12	Maintenance & Repair Construction											.00008
13	Ordnance & Accessories		.00008				.00019				.00010	.00040
14	Food & Kindred Products	.13319		.02529								
15	Tobacco Manufactures											
16	Broad & Narrow Fabrics, Yarn & Thread Mills	.00035	.00034	.03536	.02296	.00001	.00019	(*)	.00017	.00002	.00043	.00047
17	Miscellaneous Textile Goods & Floor Coverings		.00106			(*)	.00010					.00189
18	Apparel	.00065					.00001					.00044
19	Miscellaneous Fabricated Textile Products	.00008	.00158									.00011
20	Lumber & Wood Products, Except Containers		.00008	.00072	.00798	.00169	.00651	.00636	.00001		.00043	.05424
21	Wooden Containers		.00355	.00355								
22	Household Furniture											
23	Other Furniture & Fixtures	.00044	.00004		.00003	.00015	.00026	.00038	.00014	.00287	.00289	.00523
24	Paper & Allied Products, Except Containers	.00006		.00022	.04877							.00281
25	Paperboard Containers & Boxes		.00011									.00317
26	Printing & Publishing	.00018	.00032	.00020	.00001	.00002	.00005	.00002	.00003	.00004	.00005	.00007
27	Chemicals & Selected Chemical Products	.00213	.05224	.00091	.00051	.01487	.03669	.01443	.00822	.01688	.02871	.00003
28	Plastics & Synthetic Materials			(*)		(*)	.00009	(*)		.00011	.00025	.00307
29	Drugs, Cleaning & Toilet Preparations	.00310		.00252	(*)		.00001		.00037	.00001		.00002
30	Paints & Allied Products						.00001			.00001	.00002	.00003
31	Petroleum Refining & Related Industries	.00636	.03499	.01959	.00195	.00737	.00462	.00868	.00524	.02550	.00823	.01709
32	Rubber & Miscellaneous Plastics Products	.00109	.00419	.00059	.00004	.00473	.00641	.01233	.00128	.03455	.00250	.00743
33	Leather Tanning & Industrial Leather Products											.00001
34	Footwear & Other Leather Products	.00027			.00156	(*)	.00001	(*)		.00001	.00001	.00123
35	Glass & Glass Products	.00020		(*)	(*)	.00251	.00112	.00110	.00333	.05715	.00065	.08872

Note: This page is a single large numeric input–output style table (rotated on the page) with no column headings (it is a fragment continuing columns from preceding pages). The 11 numeric columns are labeled below C1–C11 in printed left-to-right order. Values are reproduced as read; blank cells are left empty; "(*)" denotes "Less than 0.000005" per the footnote.

#	Industry	C1	C2	C3	C4	C5	C6	C7	C8	C9	C10	C11
37	Primary Iron & Steel Manufacturing	.00003	.00115	.00003		.01493	.01777	.01486	.00243	.01362	.01974	.03244
38	Primary Nonferrous Metal Manufacturing	.00029		.00046		.00102	.00025	.00003	.00150	.00116	.00287	.01898
39	Metal Containers			.01216								
40	Heating, Plumbing & Structural Metal Products			.00861	.07439	.00022	.00099			.00084	.00080	.09400
41	Stampings, Screw Machine Products & Bolts	.00093	.00024	.00940	.00010	.00091	.00249	.00466	.00107	.00220	.00099	.00171
42	Other Fabricated Metal Products	.00077				.00585	.00719	.01355	.00129	.01838	.00663	.01488
43	Engines & Turbines	.00020				.01674	.01954	.03210	.00200	.02354	.02341	.00040
44	Farm Machinery & Equipment											.00002
45	Construction, Mining & Oil Field Machinery										.00636	.00364
46	Materials Handling Machinery & Equipment	.00011	.00093			.00015	.00228	.00022	.00200	.00792	.00240	.00393
47	Metalworking Machinery & Equipment		.00051			.00083	.00037	.00172	.00003		.00248	.00017
48	Special Industry Machinery & Equipment											
49	General Industrial Machinery & Equipment			.00025						.01130	.00693	.00320
50	Machine Shop Products			.00011	.00001					.00378	.00137	.00018
51	Office, Computing & Accounting Machines	.00003	.00016				.00048	.00079				
52	Service Industry Machines					.00016	.02082	.00425		.00367	.00020	.00617
53	Electric Industrial Equipment & Apparatus			.02045	.00001	.00014	.00043		.00666	.00051	.00143	.00515
54	Household Appliances				.00003		.00040		.00002			.00280
55	Electric Lighting & Wiring Equipment				.00022						.00044	.01715
56	Radio, Television & Communication Equipment	.00022	.00007		(*)	.00004	.00013	.00279	.00033		.00003	.00121
57	Electronic Components & Accessories	.00025	.01131		.01445	.00013	(*)	.00419	.00119		.05592	.00002
58	Miscellaneous Electrical Machinery, Equipment & Supplies			.00105		.00004	.00018		.00007	.00069	.00402	.00056
59	Motor Vehicles & Equipment			.00022		.00017	.00155		.00027	.00724		.00056
60	Aircraft & Parts					.00156						
61	Other Transportation Equipment	(*)	.00303		.00045	.00006	.00122	.00030	.00036	.0006	.05165	.00007
62	Scientific & Controlling Instruments	.00006			.02382	.00025	.00033	.00301	(*)	.00002	.02059	.00317
63	Optical, Ophthalmic & Photographic Equipment	.02272			.00322	.00001		.00337	.02293	.01661	.00832	.00007
64	Miscellaneous Manufacturing			.00012		.08811	.00067	(*)				.00136
65	Transportation & Warehousing			.02517		.00091	.01947	.01760				.03271
66	Communications; Except Radio & TV Broadcasting	.00196	.00749			.01868	.00115	.00134	.00070	.00030	.01622	.00275
67	Radio & TV Broadcasting	.00360	.03090			.01502						
68	Electric, Gas, Water & Sanitary Services	.03260	.01155	.00009		.00476	.02687	.02469	.01148	.03064		.00313
69	Wholesale & Retail Trade	.00583		.03215	.02324		.01827	.02199	.01180	.02669		.08323
70	Finance & Insurance			.00188			.01637	.01076	.00763	.01423		.00612
71	Real Estate & Rental	.01082	.07407			.07753	.02748	.02769	.18312	.02212		.00469
72	Hotels; Personal & Repair Services exc. Auto	.00519										
73	Business Services	.00285	.03068	.00038	.00002	.02282	.00923	.01080	.00881	.01076	.00882	.04516
75	Automobile Repair & Services		.00589	.00387	.00051	.00073	.00151	.00293	.00343	.00932	.00137	.00358
76	Amusements	.00677	.00047									
77	Medical, Educational Services & Nonprofit Organizations	.00015	.00015			.00054	.00068	.00077	.00039	.00019	.00262	.00087
78	Federal Government Enterprises	.00002	.00003	.00018	.00017	.00080	.00082	.00068	.00043	.00050	.00230	.00028
79	State & Local Government Enterprises	.00659	.01594	.00017	.00003	.00040	.00057	.00024	.00026	.00112	.00122	.00043
80	Gross Imports of Goods & Services			.24437	.00006	.29580	.14007	.06083	.08531	.05336	.12564	
81	Business Travel, Entertainment & Gifts	.00066	.00117	.01002	.00904	.00231	.00453	.00409	.00544	.00533	.00274	.00547
82	Office Supplies	.00003	.00003	.00025	.00023	.00023	.00030	.00041	.00041	.00041	.00032	.00026
83	Scrap, Used & Secondhand Goods			.00309		.00037	.00344	.00033	.00033	.00230	.00145	.00050
V.A.	Value Added	.25080	.54388	.34163	.32835	.33257	.41171	.58412	.56475	.55470	.51735	.39516
T.	Total	1.00000	1.00000	1.00000	1.00000	1.00000	1.00000	1.00000	1.00000	1.00000	1.00000	1.00000

*Less than 0.000005. Note.—Detail may not add due to rounding.
Source: U.S. Department of Commerce, Office of Business Economics

Source: *Survey of Current Business*, November, 1969, pp. 42–43.

TABLE A2—Continued

[Producers' prices]

Column industry key:
12 = Maintenance and repair construction; 13 = Ordnance and accessories; 14 = Food and kindred products; 15 = Tobacco manufactures; 16 = Broad and narrow fabrics, yarn and thread mills; 17 = Miscellaneous textile goods and floor coverings; 18 = Apparel; 19 = Miscellaneous fabricated textile products; 20 = Lumber and wood products, except containers; 21 = Wooden containers; 22 = Household furniture; 23 = Other furniture and fixtures; 24 = Paper and allied products, except containers; 25 = Paperboard containers and boxes; 26 = Printing and publishing; 27 = Chemicals and selected chemical products; 28 = Plastics and synthetic materials.

Industry No.	12	13	14	15	16	17	18	19	20	21	22	23	24	25	26	27	28
1	0.00001		0.21955		0.00356	0.04938			0.01596							0.00103	
2			.08205	0.15147	.10116	.00785	0.00640		.08596							.00167	
3			.03409														
4																	
5																.00491	
6	.01309	0.00020	.00052	.00024	.00097	.00038			.00020	0.00006	0.00037	0.00035	0.00580	0.00017	0.00004	.00501	0.00380
7																.00405	
8																	
9	.00036	.00091	.00010	.00098	.00003	.00252	.00009	0.00008	.00002				.00424	.00007		.00194	
10	.00014		.00007	.00016		.00582			.00001				.00090			.02785	.00005
11	(*)		.00200	.23753	.00224	.17659			.00334							.00477	.00384
12	.00014	.00060	.17354		.00245	.06814	.00083	.00117	.00005	.00172	.00118	.00168	.00346	.00262	.00158	.00001	.00316
13	.00066	.00253		.00011		.00793		.00005		.00017		.00005	.00939	.00006	.00025	.01429	
14	.00001					.02570								.00005	.00086		
15	.03655			.00067		.00002											
16	.00021	.00084	.00020	.00466	.32652	.00088	.27235	.39228	.00002	.00200	.05265	.00091	.00542	.00001	.00026	.00014	.00022
17	.00358	.00003	.00003	.01231	.03900	.01280	.00321	.09924	.00134		.02593	.01534	.00239	.00111	.00144	.00002	.00009
18		.00031	.00067	.00773	.00253	.00801	.17745	.01912	.00006		.00174	.00130	.00075	.00004		.00041	
19		.00050	.00138	.00030	.00342	.00077	.01557	.08555	.00165		.00054	.00041	.00143	.00082			.00048
20		.00115	.00012	.01044	.00001	.00410		.00264	.29773	.37399	.13979	.07783	.06096		.00169	.00248	.00052
21	.00005	.00021	.00118	(*)	.00001	.15190	(*)	.00078	.00227	.03174	.00002	.00037	.00005	.00045	(*)	.00025	.00028
22	.00274	.00247	(*)	.00027	.00002	.00214		.00006	.00182	.00412	.01776	.02051	.00001	.00006	.00112		
23		.00015		.00001		(*)		.00724	.00242	.00060	.00584	.02201	.17225	.00005	.16151	(*)	
24	.04338	.00009	.01215	(*)	.00405		.00060	.00891	.00165	.00554	.00083	.00083	.02990	.39800	.00560	.01191	.03350
25		(*)	.01533		.00527		.00707				.01292	.01681		.02871		.00634	.00645
26	.02728	.00210	.00606		.00007	.00225	.00009	.00012	.00013	.00011	.00011	.00019	.00791	.00850	.11102	.00013	.00010
27	.00703	.01628	.00328	.00027	.02626	.01993	.00077	.00026	.00882	.00062	.00173	.00061	.03490	.01714	.02357	.17660	.36614
28		.00004	.00138	.00001	.08305	.00008	.01932	.00897	.00153	.00015	.00170		.01397	.00817	.00210	.02051	.01577
29		(*)	.00291	(*)	.00264	.00005	.00057	.00030	.00015	.00002	.00013	.00028	.00118	.00008	.00014	.01362	.00342
30			.00001		.00054		(*)	(*)	.00483		.02235	.01860	.00003	(*)	.00146	.00384	.00348
31			.00283		.00168		.00003	.00063	.00444	.00186	.00148	.00186	.00805	.00731	.00265	.06268	.01748
32			.00342		.00220		.00158	.03216	.00127	.00036	.06227	.04698	.01404	.00251	.00440	.00166	.01638
33			.00004		.00015		.00221		.00014	.00018	.00107	.00116	.00018	.00004	.00002	.00021	.00008
34	(*)		(*)		.00006		.00087	.00153	.00132	.00076	.00001	(*)	.00004	.00003	.00003		
35	.00471		.01045		.00001			.00053			.00664	.02104		.00153		.00058	.00010

Age																	
36	.00006	.00215	(*)	(*)	.00373	.00787	.00002		.00508	.00022	(*)	.00126	.00005		.00002	(*)	.02070
37	.00002	.01343	.00010		.00012	.09426	.02266		.00434	.00087	(*)	.00006	(*)		.00003	.02350	.01603
38	.00040	.01258	.00039	.00382	.00102	.01026	.07782		.00069	.00087		.00006		.00123	.00001	.03066	.01054
39	.00227	.00022	.00009	.00700	.00002		.00002								.02145		
40	.00001	.00004		.00008	.00003	.00505	.03112	.08021	.00062	.00007	.00097	.00003				.00164	.02873
41		.00006	.00006	.00331	.00003	.01314	.03304	.00153	.00172	.00027			.00001		.00270	.00562	.00095
42		.00566	.00146	.00434	.01278	.04286	.03682	.00546	.01611	.00102		.00039	.00054	.00566	.00290	.00550	.01357
43	.00037						.00001									.00049	
44																.00003	.00003
45		.00001		.00014		.00121	.00046	.00010	.00002	.00002	.00013	.00003				.00042	.00381
46	.00020	.00044	.00011		.00042	.00016	.00021	.00048	.00038	.00014		.00011	.00020	.00003	.00009	.00014	.00484
47		.00033	.00002	.00163	.00001	.00060	.00002	.00013				.00002	.00001		.00047	.00346	.00002
48		.00878	.00202	.00004	.00222	.00019	.00003	.00423	.00306	.00037	.00039	.00303	.00574	(*)	.00006	.00015	.00218
49	.00017	.00148	.00030	.00002	.00191	.00153	.00005	.00014	.00033	.00001	.00006	.00012	.00007		.00005	.00317	.00005
50	.00001	.00002	.00004		.00002	.00163	.00003	.00003	.00007		.00001	.00001	.00001			.00210	
51		.00001				.00008			.00001	.00016					(*)	.00001	.00586
52		.00001	.00001	.00001	.00001	.00346	.00006		.00005							.00165	.00285
53	.00005	.00166		.00001		.00039	.00019			.00007						.00395	.00500
54						.00010										.00079	.00927
55	(*)	.00001	.00001		.00002	.00521	.00013	.00002	.00001	.00001	.00001	.00025	(*)	(*)	.00001	.00734	
56		.00005			.00005	.00164	.00006	.00044	.00005	.00065	.00001		.00025			.04464	.00101
57		.00003		.00007		.00159	.00074	.00015	.00008	.00004	.00002	.00006	.00008		.00009	.01679	
58	.00002	.00004	.00013	.00008	.00019	.00019	.00005	.00268	.00011	.00004		.00004	.00011	.00001	.00020	.00298	.00005
59	.00007	.00011	.00026		.00010	.00025		.04800	.00030	.00015	.00004	.00003	.01628			.00017	.00051
60	.00001		.00022		.00001	.00074	.00010		.00009							.29040	.00071
61	.00001	(*)		.00022	.00046	.00004	.00038		.00007	.00003	.00058	.00158	.00197	.00006	.00010	.00276	(*)
62	.00012	.00012	.00028	.00007	.00099	.00745	.00146		.00030	.00131	.00015	.00005	.00996	.00007	.00003	.00031	.00353
63	.00004	.00008	.00828	.00018	.00038	.00015	.00013		.00011	.00011	.01965	.01100	.03406	.00003	.00011	.00843	.00001
64	.00009	.00116	.00182	.03004	.03732	.00162	.00242		.00161	.00527	.00600	.02148	.00373	.00419	.03314	.00013	.00391
65	.01936	.02702	.01114			.01846	.02203	.00345	.03242	.06676						.00439	.02475
66	.00362	.00372	.01166	.00440	.00290	.00605	.00479	.00854	.00273	.00354	.00424	.00241	.00470	.00046	.00257	.00831	.00397
67	.01114	.03489	.00524	.00615	.02090	.00700	.00573	.02797	.00777	.00380	.00354	.00631	.00026	.00108	.00667	.00418	.04452
68	.02792	.02918	.02259	.02101	.03231	.03649	.04270	.00491	.02514	.04453	.03556	.05626	.00933	.00879	.03497	.01481	.08600
69	.00532	.00532	.00729	.00345	.00556	.01199	.00860		.00769	.00524	.00493	.00389	.00040	.00206	.00514	.00425	.00815
70																	
71	.00685	.00589	.05419	.00089	.00606	.01516	.02118	.00949	.00760	.00812	.01193	.00595	.00470	.00176	.00497	.00474	.00679
72	.00055	.00062	.00175	.00181	.00129	.00039	.00039	.00962		.00088	.00017	.00065	.00026	.00144	.00237	.00155	.00155
73	.00055	.02139	.03087	.01717	.01546	.01706	.02048	.00966	.01291	.00879	.01308	.01021	.00933	.04209	.02963	.01740	.01419
74	.02575	.00086	.00209	.00106	.00072	.00154	.00133	.00176	.00276	.00062	.00064	.00044	.00040	.00013	.00245	.00145	.08511
75	.00058																
76	.00043	.00043	.00174	.00055	.00037	.00075	.00060	.00045	.00037	.00043	.00051	.00028	.00023	.00007	.00046	.00122	.00124
77	.00053	.00179	.01105	.00085	.00082	.00161	.00129	.00083	.00056	.00161	.00256	.00100	.00080	.00174	.00069	.00165	.00040
78	.00026	.00045	.00031	.00007	.00041	.00012	.00009	.00013	.00020	.00013	.00005	.00014	.00018	.00002	.00034	.00007	.00050
79	.00927	.02426	.00040	.00196	.08354		.00013	.01144	.06337		.00306	.13137	.03179	.00991	.03306	.00286	.00286
80																	
81	.00574	.00719	.01726	.00364	.00481	.00615	.00767	.00820	.00350	.00486	.00524	.00277	.00321	.00513	.00344	.00770	.00777
82	.00051	.00075	.00270	.00083	.00064	.00135	.00107	.00082	.00051	.00071	.00097	.00048	.00065	.00022	.00065	.00162	.00038
83		.00207			.01828							.01216					
V.A.T.	.40292	.40766	.48439	.39766	.36686	.42214	.33671	.34313	.36159	.23669	.37559	.17886	.26445	.48620	.20787	.40067	.56236
	1.00000	1.00000	1.00000	1.00000	1.00000	1.00000	1.00000	1.00000	1.00000	1.00000	1.00000	1.00000	1.00000	1.00000	1.00000	1.00000	1.00000

TABLE A3 Total Requirements (Direct and Indirect) per Dollar of Delivery to Final Demand, 1963

[Producers' prices]

Each entry represents the output required, directly and indirectly, from the industry named at the beginning of the row for each dollar of delivery to final demand by the industry named at the head of the column.

Column headings:
1. Livestock and livestock products
2. Other agricultural products
3. Forestry and fishery products
4. Agricultural, forestry and fishery services
5. Iron and ferroalloy ores mining
6. Nonferrous metal ores mining
7. Coal mining
8. Crude petroleum and natural gas
9. Stone and clay mining and quarrying
10. Chemical and fertilizer mineral mining

Industry No.	Industry	1	2	3	4	5	6	7	8	9	10
1	Livestock & Livestock Products	1.31963	0.10112	0.11907	0.18536	0.00291	0.00268	0.00239	0.00483	0.02530	0.00193
2	Other Agricultural Products	.43481	1.07832	.12999	.39019	.00381	.00314	.00285	.00639	.00286	.00222
3	Forestry & Fishery Products	.00141	.00073	1.02090	.00130	.00048	.00134	.00124	.00038	.00038	.00037
4	Agricultural, Forestry & Fishery Services	.03898	.04347	.05041	1.01832	.00028	.00029	.00027	.00042	.00024	.00019
5	Iron & Ferroalloy Ores Mining	.00074	.00090	.00111	.00153	1.04173	.00375	.00242	.00063	.00233	.00470
6	Nonferrous Metal Ores Mining	.00063	.00091	.00063	.00143	.02314	1.21088	.00113	.00051	.00396	.00151
7	Coal Mining	.00182	.00156	.00120	.00187	.00653	.00433	1.18998	.00113	.00630	.00472
8	Crude Petroleum & Natural Gas	.01799	.02576	.01660	.01405	.01088	.01089	.01162	1.03246	.12066	.01430
9	Stone and Clay Mining and Quarrying	.00245	.00460	.00107	.00225	.00447	.00135	.00120	.00142	1.01508	.00900
10	Chemical & Fertilizer Mineral Mining	.00180	.00373	.00081	.00174	.00090	.00701	.00090	.00050	.00202	1.04780
11	New Construction	.02803	.02957	.00964	.01835	.01665	.01670	.01643	.05321	.01650	.01616
12	Maintenance & Repair Construction	.00008	.00007	.00009	.00015	.00012	.00016	.00023	.00011	.00026	.00018
13	Ordnance & Accessories										
14	Food & Kindred Products	.21689	.02195	.05810	.06081	.00406	.00560	.00466	.00484	.00550	.00442
15	Tobacco Manufactures	.00021	.00020	.00042	.00043	.00019	.00029	.00026	.00027	.00040	.00020
16	Broad & Narrow Fabrics, Yarn & Thread Mills	.00313	.00340	.01341	.00975	.00084	.00152	.00139	.00068	.00279	.00149
17	Miscellaneous Textile Goods & Floor Coverings	.00290	.00326	.04164	.02729	.00062	.00095	.00119	.00055	.00239	.00056
18	Apparel	.00064	.00047	.00091	.00099	.00035	.00048	.00047	.00034	.00064	.00039
19	Miscellaneous Fabricated Textile Products	.00228	.00227	.00261	.00195	.00019	.00026	.00028	.00015	.00056	.00021
20	Lumber & Wood Products, Except Containers	.00485	.00562	.00319	.01094	.00468	.01367	.01318	.00365	.00326	.00304
21	Wooden Containers	.00229	.00009	.00106	.01007	.00009	.00016	.00015	.00009	.00016	.00010
22	Household Furniture	.00010	.00009	.00021	.00027	.00006	.00010	.00012	.00006	.00009	.00006
23	Other Furniture & Fixtures	.00006	.00006	.00006	.00012	.00004	.00005	.00005	.00004	.00005	.00005
24	Paper & Allied Products, Except Containers	.01327	.00861	.00856	.03399	.00466	.00571	.00540	.00384	.01086	.00812
25	Paperboard Containers & Boxes	.00776	.00459	.00615	.05617	.00119	.00181	.00183	.00097	.00280	.00152
26	Printing & Publishing	.01370	.01342	.00678	.01021	.00076	.00764	.00753	.00646	.00814	.00669
27	Chemicals & Selected Chemical Products	.03981	.07688	.02055	.03908	.02566	.06130	.02855	.01544	.03461	.04297
28	Plastics & Synthetic Materials	.00390	.00448	.01021	.00877	.00263	.00428	.00494	.00176	.01020	.00281
29	Drugs, Cleaning & Toilet Preparations	.00646	.00227	.00164	.00225	.00090	.00143	.00095	.00078	.00136	.00140
30	Paints & Allied Products	.00197	.00207	.00412	.00200	.00117	.00147	.00145	.00305	.00154	.00132
31	Petroleum Refining & Related Industries	.03544	.05210	.03428	.02758	.01822	.01563	.01827	.01308	.03688	.01929
32	Rubber & Miscellaneous Plastics Products	.00706	.00757	.00553	.00694	.00797	.01105	.01863	.00343	.04126	.00608
33	Leather Tanning & Industrial Leather Products	.00020	.00016	.00012	.00193	.00007	.00010	.00010	.00010	.00016	.00009
34	Footwear & Other Leather Products	.00054	.00020	.00026	.00193	.00009	.00012	.00012	.00010	.00017	.00009
35	Glass & Glass Products	.00328	.00078	.00195	.00135	.00040	.00053	.00073	.00064	.00076	.00050

No.	Industry										
36	Stone & Clay Products	.00302	.06772	.00593	.00375	.00370	.00460	.00309	.00223	.00389	.00270
37	Primary Iron & Steel Manufacturing	.04263	.04014	.01031	.04418	.04617	.03139	.02813	.01917	.00951	.01035
38	Primary Nonferrous Metal Manufacturing	.01258	.01212	.00470	.00983	.01011	.00672	.01509	.00891	.00535	.00471
39	Metal Containers	.00076	.00087	.00058	.00065	.00097	.00057	.00271	.01458	.00228	.00620
40	Heating, Plumbing & Structural Metal Products	.00216	.00258	.00354	.00165	.00262	.00131	.00154	.00137	.00128	.00122
41	Stampings, Screw Machine Products & Bolts	.00201	.00319	.00097	.00285	.00224	.00143	.00294	.00231	.00134	.00299
42	Other Fabricated Metal Products	.00514	.00817	.00358	.01049	.00779	.00404	.08295	.01625	.00730	.00759
43	Engines & Turbines	.00945	.02223	.00195	.01956	.01101	.00816	.00370	.00083	.00104	.00072
44	Farm Machinery & Equipment	.00094	.00094	.00027	.00139	.00095	.00075	.00373	.00139	.00978	.04433
45	Construction, Mining & Oil Field Machinery	.02684	.02671	.02670	.04052	.02570	.01941	.00074	.00039	.00070	.00052
46	Materials Handling Machinery & Equipment	.00770	.00934	.00042	.00094	.00352	.00065	.00045	.00022	.00037	.00032
47	Metalworking Machinery & Equipment	.00252	.00364	.00076	.00559	.00394	.00260	.00187	.00104	.00078	.00068
48	Special Industry Machinery & Equipment	.00094	.00118	.00053	.00090	.00116	.00065	.00130	.00076	.00111	.00083
49	General Industrial Machinery & Equipment	.00080	.01734	.00053	.00627	.00462	.00286	.00136	.00173	.00180	.00118
50	Machine Shop Products	.00443	.00666	.00050	.00750	.02967	.00177	.00094	.00082	.00107	.00087
51	Office, Computing & Accounting Machines	.00046	.00061	.00044	.00057	.00050	.00058	.00052	.00034	.00067	.00058
52	Service Industry Machines	.00051	.00072	.00062	.00051	.00046	.00039	.00056	.00035	.00049	.00045
53	Electric Industrial Equipment & Apparatus	.01005	.00701	.00845	.00613	.00296	.00159	.00154	.00212	.00129	.00109
54	Household Appliances	.00056	.00072	.00069	.00062	.00048	.00035	.00071	.00058	.00043	.00041
55	Electric Lighting & Wiring Equipment	.00209	.00126	.00084	.00568	.00102	.00060	.00057	.02199	.00062	.00062
56	Radio, Television & Communication Equipment	.00084	.00125	.00102	.00106	.00099	.00066	.00070	.00061	.00052	.00052
57	Electronic Components & Accessories	.00080	.00089	.00193	.00076	.00079	.00048	.00063	.00072	.00041	.00042
58	Miscellaneous Electrical Machinery, Equipment & Supplies	.00111	.00213	.00053	.00160	.00115	.00097	.00111	.00249	.00168	.00137
59	Motor Vehicles & Equipment	.00552	.01567	.00204	.00921	.00585	.00504	.00301	.00285	.00302	.00311
60	Aircraft & Parts	.00131	.00186	.00058	.00166	.00135	.00134	.00132	.00081	.00051	.00071
61	Other Transportation Equipment	.00157	.00110	.00051	.00535	.00248	.00126	.00069	.01371	.00062	.00067
62	Scientific & Controlling Instruments	.00075	.00104	.00103	.00087	.00139	.00077	.00091	.00102	.00049	.00059
63	Optical, Ophthalmic & Photographic Equipment	.00146	.00053	.00040	.00046	.00046	.00048	.00058	.00040	.00061	.00063
64	Miscellaneous Manufacturing	.00102	.00167	.00104	.00124	.00209	.00112	.00208	.00169	.00158	.00159
65	Transportation & Warehousing	.07874	.04034	.03689	.03795	.04261	.11195	.04894	.05176	.03203	.05962
66	Communications; Except Radio & TV Broadcasting	.00801	.00479	.00384	.00531	.00544	.00504	.00621	.00390	.00793	.00910
67	Radio & TV Broadcasting	.00143	.00176	.00139	.00165	.00163	.00234	.00199	.00117	.00316	.00271
68	Electric, Gas, Water & Sanitary Services	.07696	.05182	.02054	.04521	.05121	.03317	.01695	.01031	.02173	.02165
69	Wholesale & Retail Trade	.03670	.04712	.02735	.04167	.03814	.03059	.06494	.05991	.05503	.06091
70	Finance & Insurance	.01822	.02611	.02097	.02278	.03172	.01610	.02038	.01168	.02563	.02567
71	Real Estate & Rental	.03058	.03873	.20300	.04565	.04684	.09630	.07187	.02556	.10152	.06725
72	Hotels; Personal & Repair Services exc. Auto.	.00146	.00212	.00200	.00181	.00194	.00157	.00305	.00263	.00182	.00236
73	Business Services	.02296	.02814	.02192	.02645	.02606	.03737	.03180	.01877	.05064	.04330
75	Automobile Repair & Services	.00396	.01180	.00543	.00539	.00382	.00375	.00682	.00715	.00885	.00951
76	Amusements	.00083	.00107	.00117	.00100	.00101	.00128	.00136	.00094	.00164	.00145
77	Medical, Educational Services & Nonprofit Organizations	.00344	.00106	.00118	.00164	.00168	.00129	.00231	.00147	.00200	.01012
78	Federal Government Enterprises 1	.00567	.00376	.00303	.00367	.00417	.00375	.00323	.00224	.00358	.00384
79	State & Local Government Enterprises	.01383	.00977	.00571	.00785	.00917	.00859	.00455	.00348	.00497	.00555
80	Gross Imports of Goods & Services	.14571	.06975	.09393	.01286	.18303	.32309	.02899	.27063	.03137	.03454
81	Business Travel, Entertainment & Gifts	.00995	.01066	.00868	.00905	.00998	.00638	.04505	.01470	.00658	.00727
82	Office Supplies	.00129	.00157	.00123	.00145	.00151	.00114	.00136	.00103	.00113	.00134

*Less than 0.000005.

1. To remove a source of instability in the measurement of total requirements per dollar of delivery to final demand, the Commodity Credit Corporation has been excluded from this industry. The excluded inputs to the CCC from the specified industries are: Industry 2, $636 million; Industry 14, $214 million; Industry 16, $15 million; Industry 65, $642 million; Industry 69, $24 million; and value added, −$1,531 million.

[Producers' prices]

Industry No.	11 New construction	12 Maintenance and repair construction	13 Ordnance and accessories	14 Food and kindred products	15 Tobacco manufactures	16 Broad and narrow fabrics, yarn and thread mills	17 Miscellaneous textile goods and floor coverings	18 Apparel	19 Miscellaneous fabricated textile products	20 Lumber and wood products, except containers	21 Wooden containers	22 Household furniture	23 Other furniture and fixtures	24 Paper and allied products, except containers	25 Paperboard containers and boxes	26 Printing and publishing	27 Chemicals and selected chemical products
1	0.00480	0.00411	0.00302	0.36547	0.02177	0.03133	0.08039	0.01391	0.02425	0.01888	0.00931	0.00982	0.00632	0.00826	0.00492	0.00635	0.00094
2	.01116	.00479	.00310	.22885	.21608	.17425	.07089	.06257	.08580	.04265	.01866	.02087	.00862	.00968	.00565	.00667	.00893
3	.00742	.00498	.00079	.00609	.00049	.00082	.00102	.00854	.00131	.12549	.04878	.01848	.01097	.00988	.00443	.00239	.00310
4	.00104	.00063	.00027	.01524	.00878	.00742	.00427	.00314	.00393	.00737	.00304	.00314	.00101	.00102	.00057	.00055	.00073
5	.00506	.00258	.00350	.00132	.00046	.00114	.00108	.00066	.00091	.00128	.00608	----	.00776	.00103	.00103	.00065	.00789
6	.00461	.00286	.00713	.00070	.00043	.00131	.00128	.00080	.00110	.00094	.00108	.00258	.00321	.00120	.00140	.00080	.01104
7	.00456	.00247	.00295	.00285	.00134	.00472	.00400	.00256	.00345	.00201	.00416	.00351	.00560	.01087	.00562	.00317	.00925
8	.00648	.02044	.00648	.01947	.00727	.01555	.01403	.00884	.01138	.01072	.00936	.00906	.00870	.01448	.01346	.00858	.05013
9	.01705	.01629	.00100	.00198	.00119	.00170	.00144	.00088	.00130	.00151	.00125	.00135	.00251	.00656	.00319	.00170	.00417
10	.00106	.00095	.00063	.00142	.00110	.00414	.00368	.00193	.00264	.00095	.00064	.00133	.00109	.00337	.00228	.00182	.03636
11	1.00000	.00960	.00660	.01034	.00089	.01699	.01559	.01149	.01449	.01365	.01413	.01281	.01268	.01482	.01418	.01495	.02008
12	.01160	.00024	1.03253	.00011	.00006	.00009	.00010	.00008	.00011	.00011	.00014	.00019	.00031	.00011	.00017	.00042	.00014
13	.00053	.00992	.00794	1.28311	.00905	.01824	.02348	.01134	.01473	.01257	.01007	.01120	.00909	.02125	.01243	.01514	.03071
14	.00882	.00042	.00053	.00032	.00032	.00033	.00033	.00038	.00042	.00030	.00044	.00046	.00041	.00033	.00032	.00073	.00042
15	.00043	----	----	----	1.31395	----	----	----	----	----	----	----	----	----	----	----	----
16	.00464	.00219	.00327	.00422	.00125	1.52620	.31581	.52160	.70319	.00385	.00363	.09501	.01422	.01470	.00726	.00461	.00264
17	.00424	.00149	.00188	.00227	.00096	.06595	1.09195	.02992	.11969	.00595	.00289	.03736	.02506	.00572	.00280	.00345	.00107
18	.00165	.00153	.00193	.00164	.00028	.06606	.01296	1.21936	.02992	.00290	.00397	.00399	.00306	.00194	.00243	.00071	.00115
19	.00081	.00038	.00034	.00281	.00058	.00831	.03268	.02305	1.10267	.00071	.00047	.00344	.00160	.00246	.00122	.00072	.00151
20	.08342	.05550	.00789	.00749	.00446	.00528	.00696	.00446	.01017	1.42930	.55485	.20852	.12357	.10995	.04843	.02516	.00945
21	.00575	.00039	.00124	.00269	.00185	.00092	.00054	.00042	.00057	.00367	1.03428	.00104	.00103	.00050	.00075	.00020	.00051
22	.00313	.00029	.00132	.00017	.00006	.00020	.00114	.00021	.00117	.00278	.00547	1.01889	.02195	.00030	.00024	.00015	.00010
23	.01612	.00144	.00144	.00008	.00006	.00005	.00006	.00005	.00013	.00013	.00011	.00621	1.02276	.00008	.00013	.00135	.00006
24	.00488	.01252	.01030	.03992	.02494	.02806	.04303	.02108	.03663	.01174	.01164	.22072	.02104	1.24011	.51828	.23665	.03047
25		.00387	.00492	.02541	.01926	.01387	.01730	.01583	.02061	.00519	.00919	.02016	.02421	.04136	1.05608	.01582	.01069
26	.01854	.01007	.01340	.02758	.02952	.01249	.01345	.01221	.01311	.00982	.01006	.01364	.01291	.02210	.02659	1.14903	.01419
27	.02278	.02736	.01817	.03247	.02633	.13208	.12058	.06201	.08459	.02802	.01743	.04153	.03108	.07372	.06008	.05367	1.24310
28	.00744	.00891	.00861	.00643	.01615	.14515	.20591	.07744	.10510	.00659	.00405	.03393	.02019	.02649	.02160	.01084	.02940
29	.00186	.00182	.00134	.00660	.00223	.00774	.00705	.00442	.00527	.00143	.00129	.00243	.00209	.00353	.00243	.00223	.01922
30	.00779	.04534	.00169	.00238	.00095	.00298	.00258	.00182	.00223	.00859	.00412	.02591	.02197	.00210	.00608	.00304	.00668
31	.03160	.04109	.01073	.02498	.01401	.02752	.02517	.01532	.01969	.01956	.01587	.01556	.01436	.02425	.02401	.01476	.09323
32	.01539	.01280	.02889	.00985	.00307	.01151	.03243	.00975	.04773	.00546	.00481	.07310	.05809	.02204	.01339	.01136	.00674
33	.00024	.00016	.00024	.00020	.00010	.00030	.00042	.00384	.00074	.00041	.00067	.00165	.00176	.00044	.00030	.00022	.00045
34	.00024	.00021	.00026	.00030	.00015	.00020	.00038	.00141	.00205	.00037	.00108	.00041	.00033	.00025	.00023	.00030	.00017
35	.00380	.00641	.00268	.01500	.00039	.00597	.00209	.00247	.00388	.00270	.00142	.00890	.02453	.00100	.00057	.00094	.00188

#																	
36	.10439	.02713	.00412	.00267	.00133	.00240	.00374	.00155	.00272	.00988	.00491	.00450	.01362	.00783	.00408	.00249	.00544
37	.09410	.04725	.06616	.02287	.00621	.00876	.00883	.00662	.00919	.02224	.12060	.05817	.15212	.01232	.01390	.00703	.02813
38	.05693	.03153	.09180	.00603	.00340	.00621	.00685	.00533	.00734	.00967	.01095	.02980	.03742	.00937	.01320	.00595	.03064
39	.00143	.00369	.00073	.02888	.00255	.00267	.00276	.00155	.00194	.00284	.00147	.00289	.00243	.00201	.00871	.00144	.01373
40	.09825	.03088	.00335	.00107	.00053	.00110	.00101	.00074	.00102	.00202	.00157	.00282	.00706	.00113	.00105	.00086	.00149
41	.00755	.00446	.01696	.00566	.00076	.00109	.00146	.00119	.00174	.00408	.00469	.00690	.01826	.00166	.00489	.00111	.00183
42	.02856	.02097	.01949	.00877	.01029	.00483	.00489	.00452	.00553	.02842	.02060	.07923	.05634	.02119	.01478	.00737	.01096
43	.00227	.00128	.00260	.00074	.00051	.00070	.00061	.00046	.00057	.00061	.00072	.00074	.00094	.00083	.00066	.00052	.00134
44	.00081	.00056	.00056	.00237	.00215	.00178	.00090	.00077	.00101	.00064	.00056	.00106	.00192	.00031	.00028	.00052	.00042
45	.00621	.00522	.00149	.00053	.00031	.00074	.00064	.00043	.00057	.00058	.00079	.00084	.00112	.00104	.00068	.00049	.00223
46	.00516	.00578	.00096	.00041	.00021	.00071	.00058	.00054	.00065	.00087	.00109	.00078	.00075	.00097	.00070	.00048	.00124
47	.00367	.00216	.01681	.00085	.00047	.00100	.00089	.00063	.00086	.01122	.00176	.00228	.00362	.00109	.00095	.00071	.00196
48	.00151	.00108	.00140	.00145	.00056	.01117	.00704	.00468	.00606	.00534	.00723	.00258	.00204	.00450	.00414	.00391	.01215
49	.00788	.00521	.00974	.00126	.00071	.00180	.00159	.00113	.00179	.00191	.00236	.00216	.00459	.00388	.00223	.00171	.00408
50	.00244	.00144	.02136	.00084	.00036	.00062	.00055	.00042	.00057	.00079	.00156	.00127	.00402	.00064	.00062	.00049	.00131
51	.00111	.00067	.00116	.00081	.00083	.00064	.00062	.00057	.00083	.00055	.00055	.00079	.00084	.00057	.00058	.00073	.00075
52	.00909	.00741	.00291	.00048	.00037	.00038	.00039	.00032	.00039	.00050	.00051	.00069	.00459	.00043	.00039	.00043	.00051
53	.01158	.00705	.01140	.00131	.00080	.00154	.00149	.00116	.00147	.00148	.00210	.00226	.00406	.00147	.00128	.00119	.00450
54	.00468	.00038	.00261	.00044	.00030	.00043	.00048	.00043	.00049	.00050	.00055	.00101	.00129	.00048	.00044	.00055	.00059
55	.01895	.01041	.01059	.00064	.00026	.00051	.00081	.00061	.00057	.00313	.00058	.00115	.00654	.00074	.00055	.00054	.00079
56	.00283	.00222	.07090	.00061	.00037	.00056	.00070	.00059	.00081	.00066	.00075	.00068	.00347	.00063	.00052	.00089	.00079
57	.00168	.00124	.03478	.00057	.00035	.00046	.00065	.00052	.00136	.00062	.00041	.00054	.00310	.00052	.00054	.00068	.00069
58	.00235	.00172	.00559	.00109	.00054	.00070	.00066	.00050	.00062	.00101	.00104	.00081	.00126	.00071	.00068	.00065	.00072
59	.00583	.00479	.00529	.00304	.00114	.00178	.00174	.00139	.00175	.00298	.00331	.00210	.00454	.00204	.00065	.00196	.00243
60	.00182	.00121	.36639	.00096	.00035	.00067	.00085	.00059	.00104	.00101	.00007	.00094	.00242	.00089	.00103	.00103	.00086
61	.00196	.00100	.00399	.00082	.00032	.00062	.00066	.00059	.00061	.00241	.00140	.00057	.00098	.00087	.00075	.00052	.00081
62	.00546	.00504	.01524	.00070	.00039	.00103	.00254	.00141	.00256	.00105	.00279	.00034	.00956	.00120	.00099	.00099	.00089
63	.00109	.00067	.01133	.00102	.00096	.00085	.00086	.00096	.00103	.00071	.00101	.00085	.00106	.00202	.00141	.01103	.00085
64	.00432	.00608	.00278	.06220	.00159	.00281	.01532	.02802	.01084	.00396	.00612	.00564	.00500	.00241	.00216	.00451	.00323
65	.07079	.05183	.03132	.07633	.02202	.05366	.05850	.03679	.04788	.06941	.05893	.09664	.05506	.07337	.07393	.04601	.06474
66	.01075	.00941	.01684	.01045	.00526	.00996	.00963	.01098	.01146	.00808	.00965	.00864	.01276	.01069	.01849		.00076
67	.00452	.00220	.00279	.00413	.00459	.00267	.00266	.00254	.00268	.00210	.00208	.00239	.00263	.00262	.00341		.00303
68	.02585	.02030	.02132	.02632	.01057	.03723	.03104	.02340	.03040	.02308	.02817	.04529	.02852	.03227	.02286		.06880
69	.11590	.11000	.04632	.08334	.03013	.08465	.10411	.08292	.10711	.05897	.06356	.06178	.07018	.05605	.04973		.05823
70	.02074	.01085	.01481	.02311	.01144	.01927	.01850	.01823	.02157	.02116	.02028	.01757	.02689	.01586	.02015		.01889
71	.03018	.02754	.02121	.04716	.03066	.03943	.03431	.03730	.03869	.02799	.03058	.04332	.03537				.03379
72	.00344	.00298	.00604	.00565	.00426	.00298	.00346	.00301	.00424	.00207	.00342	.04681	.00339				.00368
73	.07255	.03521	.04482	.06623	.07370	.04282	.04261	.04076	.04296	.03366	.03350	.00493	.04227				.04869
74	.00778	.00823	.00417	.00861	.00298	.00441	.00422	.00360	.00434	.00711	.00493						.00404
75																	
76	.00230	.00138	.00166	.00206	.00216	.00149	.00149	.00148	.00159	.00120	.00133	.00170	.00162	.00142	.00219	.00134	.00168
77	.00205	.00216	.00265	.00409	.00092	.00153	.00189	.00163	.00180	.00138	.00155	.00176	.00190	.00155	.00300	.00135	.00155
78	.00491	.00381	.00524	.00503	.00514	.00502	.00527	.00678	.00636	.00356	.00416	.00519	.00539	.00453	.01605	.00453	.00628
79	.00672	.00541	.00428	.00679	.00247	.00739	.00669	.00495	.00643	.00574	.00709	.00585	.00612	.00701	.00561	.00893	.00189
80	.03107	.02211	.02694	.06481	.02476	.07714	.17522	.03994	.06070	.13434	.07621	.04493	.03754	.06221	.03303	.12767	.06063
81	.01482	.01452	.01890	.01116	.01143	.01163	.01143	.01342	.01457	.01063	.01555	.01606	.01422	.01134	.02568	.01169	.01478
82	.00186	.00163	.00326	.00211	.00100	.00221	.00204	.00257	.00259	.00174	.00222	.00260	.00291	.00221	.00426	.00193	.00207

NOTE.—To prevent requirements for scrap and by-products from generating production, scrap and by-products have been treated as inputs to the producing industry rather than to the consuming industry.

Source: U.S. Department of Commerce, Office of Business Economics.

chapter
—7—

Regression Analysis in Business Forecasting

INTRODUCTION

By no means unique to forecasting, regression analysis is a very useful statistical tool which may be used in a wide variety of analytical situations. Regression is often misused as well. With modern computing machinery it is all too easy to take a "black box" approach, thowing all available data into the hopper and then trying all combinations to see which is "best."

Students and experienced managers alike find that the output of a regression analysis gives the illusion of being something very solid upon which to base a forecast. If well done, regression analysis may certainly lead to reliable forecasts. But there are pitfalls which the user must avoid.

At the other extreme, it is easy to take the view that forecasting is an art and not suited to the rigid logic of the regression technique. Or, after an unsuccessful try or two at the computer, the student may decide that the technique is much too complicated and cumbersome for use in forecasting. Neither position is well founded.

Modeling the Forecast

The form of the regression analysis depends on the variable to be forecast. If the forecast is to be macroeconomic in nature, there is a body of economic theory which guides the forecaster in building a model of many variables and a series of simultaneous linear equations. Models exist with as few as ten variables and equations and also with as many as 650 variables and equations.

At the level of the firm, regression analysis may be used in forecasting sales either in total or on a product-by-product basis. Microeconomic theory serves as a guide for choosing variables which influence sales of a given product. Such variables might be price, income, prices of other products, advertising effort, etc. Regression analysis may be used to determine what the influence of the variables listed might be on the sales of the product. Using the regression technique, the forecaster seeks to discover those variables which have the greatest impact on the sales of the product. Hopefully, the independent variables are either under the control of the firm or more easily forecast than the sales of the product. Using the known or forecast values of the independent variables, the forecaster then uses the equation determined by regression analysis to forecast the variables of interest, in this case the sales of a particular product.

The key to regression analysis in business forecasting is the construction of a formal model which will serve the forecaster. The importance of a model can hardly be overstated. The choice of data is guided by the model, for without hypotheses it is impossible to even identify data as distinct from numbers. Further, without some kind of model, the output of regression analysis is nothing more than a collection of numbers, and interpretation is impossible.

This is not to say that there is no interaction between the

model and empirical analysis. A model, once constructed, needs to be tested by empirical analysis. If the data contradict the model, then a new model must be developed. On the other hand, familiarity with the data will be helpful to the forecaster in constructing a model. What is to be avoided, however, is the "black box" approach.

Estimation by Regression

If the forecasting model constructed is such that the parameters of the model may be estimated by regression analysis, the forecaster then may use this powerful tool. The idea behind it is very simple. The forecaster is interested in the level some variable will assume in the future. From economic theory he knows that the level of the variable he wishes to forecast is caused by or is at least associated with the level of other variables.

In an ideal world this relationship would be as neat as the straight-line graphs drawn in economic theory texts. In the real world, when the forecaster goes to the historical record and plots the points observed on a graph, he sees that he cannot connect his observations by a single straight line. The forecaster should not be dismayed by this. He knows that in the real world many things cause minor deviations from a relationship otherwise thought to exist. If he feels these disturbing forces are on balance small, as likely to push one way as another, and in general unpredictable, then he may well be satisfied with knowing the relationship which comes as close as possible to the observed data points. What regression analysis does for the forecaster is to compute a line (plane, hyperplane) which comes closer to connecting the observed points than any other line (plane, hyperplane) which could be drawn. An hyperplane or hypersurface is analogous to the plane in three dimensions, in that it is a linear relationship among any number of variables in a like number of dimensions. It is, of course, impossible to draw on paper.

It is clearly beyond the scope of a forecasting book to discuss at length the concepts of regression analysis. Such a discussion may be readily found in statistics, econometrics, or other books designed for such a purpose. However, since an understanding of what regression is and what it can and cannot do is important to the forecaster, a brief introduction to the theory of regression is included below.

Also improper for discusssion here would be detailed computational procedures. The reader will quickly note, however, that numerical examples supplement the theoretical discussion. Since there will be some interest in how the numbers were obtained, a minimum amount of computational detail must be included, though much of it is relegated to footnote status.

There is little reason to acquire familiarity with the computation of a regression equation beyond an understanding of what is being done when the least-squares regression analysis is carried out by an electronic computer. Almost every computer installation has a regression program in its library. If not, the appropriate program could be easily obtained from the computer manufacturer.

If the forecaster is to use the regression analysis, he will have to become familiar with his own computer installation. Since the mechanics of using a computer vary with the make of computer and even with the particular installation of similar computers, the discussion here will focus instead on the model, data, and interpretation of output. In an example used below, the output of one widely used regression program will be utilized. The reader will have to relate the discussion to the output of his own machine if it differs.

While the concepts of regression set out above are simple enough, regression analysis does require some knowledge of the underlying principles. The nature of the technique imposes restrictions on the forecaster. To demonstrate exactly what regression can and cannot do, a simple linear regression model followed by a multiple linear regression model will be presented. In the process some economic theory will be reviewed. Then some of the problems faced by the forecaster in using regression analysis will be discussed. Suggestions will be made for overcoming the difficulties.

Regression Theory

Regression analysis may be used to estimate the relationship between any two or more random variables. Presumably, there would not even have to be a theoretical basis for a relationship to exist. As mentioned above, a model is very helpful. Otherwise, it is all too easy to describe the relationship between sunspot activity and business conditions or the length of women's skirts and the Dow-Jones index.

Two-Variable Model

To illustrate a two-variable regression analysis, a familiar model from microeconomics will be used. It is the simple price-quantity relationship usually referred to as a demand curve. In real-world situations, a model with such simple specifications would probably not yield acceptable forecasts. The simple demand analysis is used here as a means of illustrating part of the regression analysis. A model with somewhat more complete specifications is used later to demonstrate multiple linear regression. Regression theory is developed in terms of the relevant application. The approach remains heuristic throughout, with few formal proofs.

Suppose that a firm has observed the price and quantity combinations for its product shown in Table 7–1. Further, assume that they believe business conditions will be the same in the future as they are at the moment, so the firm is willing to prepare a forecast based on these data. Since there is no indication that the data are a time series, naive forecasts, such as the most recent level or the most recent change, are not possible. One possible forecast would be the average quantity, which is 2,767,000 gallons. But, as can be seen from the table, the estimate of σ is 607,000 gallons, which means that the forecaster may say only that there are two chances in three that the sales will be between 2,160,000 and 3,374,000 gallons. This suggests that observations on quantity alone result in a rather poor forecast.

The data from Table 7–1 may be plotted in the manner

TABLE 7–1
Price per Gallon and Gallons of Whale Oil Sold

	Price/Gal. p_i	Gallons (000) q_i	$G - \overline{G}$	$(G - \overline{G})^2$
a...................	$0.20	2,500	−267	71,289
b...................	.21	2,450	−327	106,939
c...................	.25	2,000	−767	588,289
d...................	.17	3,100	333	109,889
e...................	.15	3,750	983	965,489
f...................	.19	2,800	33	1,089
				1,842,984

$$\bar{p} = \$0.195 \quad \bar{q} = 2,767$$

$$s = \sqrt{\frac{1,842,984}{6 - 1}} \approx 607$$

shown in Figure 7–1. If the points plotted were to be connected, something very much like the demand curves shown in economic texts would result. Visual inspection of the scatter diagram reveals that a forecaster might be able to improve his forecast if he based the forecast on some knowledge of the price.

For example, if he knew that price was to be $.23, he would predict sales of 2,200,000 gallons, while he would forecast sales of 3,400,000 gallons if the price were to be $.16.

TWO-VARIABLE REGRESSION ANALYSIS

While a scatter diagram such as Figure 7–1 is always advisable as a first step in regression analysis, it may not always be possible to ascertain the relationship between the variables

FIGURE 7–1

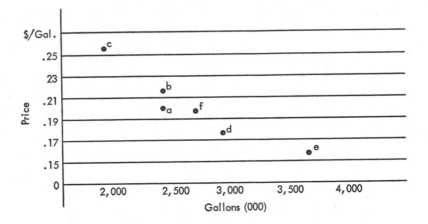

by inspection alone. It may be necessary to know precisely the equation for a straight line which most nearly connects the points in the scatter diagram. Regression analysis enables the forecaster to obtain an estimate of such a line.

Visual inspection of a scatter diagram may reveal that there is no relationship between the variables, that the relationship is other than the one hypothesized, or that the relationship is nonlinear. Further, if the letters in Figure 7–1 are replaced with dates, the forecaster may become aware of the existence of serial correlation or structural shifts in the economy. These matters will be discussed more fully in the pages to follow.

Suppose the forecaster has a theory of demand for whale oil of the form

$$q = \alpha + \beta p + u$$
$$E(u) = 0$$ '7-1)

In words this equation says that the number of gallons of whale oil (q) is a linear function of the price (p) except for some error (u). These errors might arise from a number of causes which the forecaster cannot control or even identify. Each of the errors is believed small, and in total they cancel out [$E(u) = 0$]. The parameters α and β simply describe the straight line in terms of the vertical intercept and the slope.

To perceive the regression process, it will be useful to replot the scatter diagram again, this time with the axis reversed to correspond to the equation above. The data plotted are the same as in Figure 7-1, but some additional information has been added in anticipation of the discussion to follow.

The parameters α and β represent the hypothesized true relationship between the variables. The forecaster does not know what the relationship is. Instead, he must estimate what the true value of the parameters is by using regression analysis to fit the equation

$$\hat{q} = a + bp$$ (7-2)

where $\hat{q}$ is the forecast or predicted value of q for any p given that a and b are appropriately computed. The a and b parameters will define a line. The goal of regression analysis is to define a line which most closely represents all of the points. More formally, the object is to draw a line such that the total errors (the $u_i = q_i - \hat{q}_i$) are as small as possible. No line could be constructed which would come closer to passing through each of the data points.

In Figure 7-2 u_e and u_d are indicated by brackets. The regression line has already been drawn in to demonstrate the

FIGURE 7–2

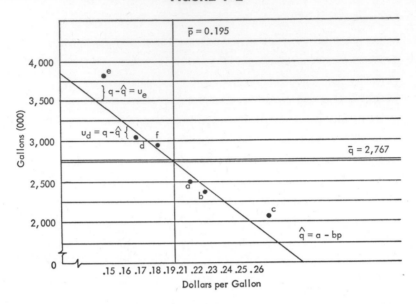

meaning of the u_i. Notice that the signs of the u_i may be plus or minus. Since the goal is to force the u_i to be as near zero as possible, the minimization must really be performed on the absolute value of the u_i. But this is difficult operationally. Thus the usual procedure is to square the u_i so that the signs are all positive. Then minimization is unambiguous. The problem becomes

$$\min \Sigma u_i^2 = \Sigma(q_i - \hat{q}_i)^2 = \Sigma(q_i - a - bp_i)^2 \qquad (7\text{–}3)$$

The result of the regression procedure[1] is

$$\hat{q} = 6076.7 - 16974.9p \qquad (7\text{–}4)$$

_____

[1] The procedure for minimization is to take the partial derivatives of Σu_i^2 with respect to a and b and set them equal to zero.

$$\frac{\partial \Sigma u_i^2}{\partial a} = 2(-1)\Sigma(q_i - a - bp_i) = 0 \qquad (1)$$

$$\frac{\partial \Sigma u_i^2}{\partial b} = 2(-1)\Sigma p_i(q_i - a - bp_i) = 0 \qquad (2)$$

Dividing both equations by -2 and moving the summation signs inside

TABLE 7–2

Observation	Price p	Gallons (000) q	Gallons Predicted (000) $\hat{q}$	$(q - q)$ Error Using Mean as Forecast	$(q - \hat{q})$ Error Using Regression Equation by Forecast
(1)	(2)	(3)	(4)	(5)	(6)
e	.15	3750	3531	983	219
d	.17	3100	3191	333	− 91
f	.19	2800	2852	33	− 52
a	.20	2500	2682	−267	−182
b	.21	2450	2512	−327	− 62
c	.25	2000	1833	−767	167

This equation should enable the forecaster to predict the quantity sold with smaller errors than if he used just the average. Table 7–2 below shows the comparison. Entries in column 6 are smaller than entries in column 5 in all but one case, and overall they sum to zero.

---

the parentheses gives a pair of simultaneous equations which, when solved for a and b, will yield a minimum Σu_i^2.

$$\Sigma q_i - na - b\Sigma p_i = 0 \qquad (3)$$
$$\Sigma p_i q_i - a\Sigma p_i - b\Sigma p_i^2 = 0 \qquad (4)$$

Equations (3) and (4) are called the normal equations. The numerical value of all of the terms except a and b is known from the sample. Two equations may be solved for the two unknowns. From Table 7–1, $n = 6$; $\Sigma q_i = 16,000$; $\Sigma p_i = 1.17$; $\Sigma p_i q_i = 3136$ and $\Sigma p_i^2 = .2341$. The solutions are:

$$a = \frac{\begin{vmatrix} 16,000 & 1.17 \\ 3136 & .2341 \end{vmatrix}}{\begin{vmatrix} 6 & 1.17 \\ 1.17 & .2341 \end{vmatrix}} = \frac{16.600(.2341) - 1.17(3136)}{6(.2341) - (1.17)^2} = 6076.7$$

$$b = \frac{\begin{vmatrix} 6 & 16,600 \\ 1.17 & 3136 \end{vmatrix}}{\begin{vmatrix} 6 & 1.17 \\ 1.17 & .2341 \end{vmatrix}} = \frac{6(3136) - 1.17(16,600)}{6(.2341) - (1.17)^2} = -16974.7$$

THE COEFFICIENT OF DETERMINATION

In addition to the regression coefficients, a useful statistic for the forecaster is the coefficient of determination. A rough definition of this statistic is that it tells how well the regression explains or fits the observed data. While a high coefficient of determination is not the only goal of the forecaster, a high coefficient of determination does lead to a greater feeling of security with respect to the forecasts produced.

The domain of this statistic is from zero to one. If the coefficient of determination is close to one, the regression relationship explains most of the variance. Or, what amounts to the same thing, the higher the value of the coefficient of determination, the less variation in the data remains which is explainable by still other variables about which the forecaster may know absolutely nothing.

The coefficient computed is the ratio of explained variance to total variance. In the above example total variance, $\Sigma(q - \bar{q})^2$, was calculated in Table 7–1 to be 1,842,984. One may calculate, from Table 7–2 above, the regression line, $\Sigma(q - \hat{q})^2$, by squaring each of the entries in column 6 and adding the results. The total is 123,803. If the regression line had gone right through all the data points, $\Sigma(q - \hat{q})^2$ would be zero. The closer the line comes to the data points, the smaller is $\Sigma(q - \hat{q})^2$. Since $\Sigma(q - \hat{q})^2$ is the unexplained variance, the ratio must be subtracted from one to yield the coefficient of determination. That is

$$r^2 = 1 - \frac{\Sigma(q - \hat{q})^2}{\Sigma(q - \bar{q})^2} \qquad (7\text{–}5)$$

In the present example

$$r^2 = 1 - \frac{123,803}{1,842,984} = .933 \qquad (7\text{–}6)$$

Thus, the regression has "explained" 93.3 percent of the variance in the dependent variable. Less than 7 percent of the variation in quantity is due to the force of variables other than price. To forecast the quantity to be sold, the forecaster need only choose the price to be charged, insert it in the formula, and calculate the quantity.

MULTIPLE LINEAR REGRESSION ANALYSIS

While the simple regression analysis has provided some insight into the reaction of quantity of whale oil sold to the price charged, the 6.7 percent unexplained variance could be troublesome to the forecaster. A technique which would allow him to introduce additional explanatory variables would be helpful to reduce the unexplained variance. Multiple regression, a simple extension of the two-variable case, is such a technique.

From the economic theory it is known that the quantity of a commodity sold depends not only on its own price but on population, advertising expenditures, prices for close substitutes and complements, and income. For the moment, suppose that theoretical considerations lead the forecaster to use a model of the form

$$q = q(p, I) \qquad (7\text{-}7)$$

where I refers to some variable, say disposable personal income. Further, suppose that a scatter diagram convinces the forecaster that the relationship is linear in all dimensions. Thus he is willing to use multiple regression analysis in the following form:

$$q = a + b_1 p + b_2 I + u \qquad (7\text{-}8)$$

This is the equation for a plane, and the intent is to orient the plane in such a way that it comes as close as possible to all the sample points. The procedure, as before, is to minimize the sum of the squared deviations between the data points and the regression plane. That is

$$\min \Sigma u^2 = \Sigma(q - \hat{q})^2 = \Sigma(q - a - b_1p - b_2I)^2. \quad (7\text{--}9)$$

Solution of the above problem will give estimates of a, b_1, and b_2, which define a plane.[2] If the forecaster knows or can forecast price and income, then he can prepare forecasts of the quantity which will be sold. If income influences the sale of whale oil, then some of the 6.7 percent unexplained variance should be explained by the variance of income.

If income does indeed influence the quantity of whale oil sold, then the coefficient b_2 will tell the forecaster something about the nature of the influence. The unexplained variance should be reduced, so that the forecaster should be able to improve his forecast of sales.

By simple extension, more than three variables may be incorporated into a multiple regression model. It is almost impossible to picture graphically more than three dimensions, but conceptually there is no problem. The forecaster may well have a model which indicates that the variable he is attempting to forecast may be influenced by two, three, or more independent variables. Multiple regression analysis enables him to study such relationships. But the introduction of three or more variables into the model introduces also a number of considerations which do not exist in the two-variable case.

---

[2] As before, the minimization proceeds:

$$\frac{\partial \Sigma u^2}{\partial a} = -2\Sigma(q - a - b_1p - b_2I) = 0 \qquad (1)$$

$$\frac{\partial \Sigma u^2}{\partial b_1} = -2\Sigma p(q - a - b_1p - b_2I) = 0 \qquad (2)$$

$$\frac{\partial \Sigma u^2}{\partial b_2} = -2\Sigma I(q - a - b_1p - b_2I) = 0 \qquad (3)$$

The normal equations are:

$$\Sigma q - na - b_1\Sigma q - b_2\Sigma I = 0 \qquad (4)$$
$$\Sigma pq - a\Sigma p - b_1\Sigma p^2 - b_2\Sigma pI = 0 \qquad (5)$$
$$\Sigma qI - a\Sigma I - b_1\Sigma pI - b_2\Sigma I^2 = 0 \qquad (6)$$

A numerical solution will not be given here. As in the two-variable case, the numerical value of all terms except a, b_1, and b_2 is known from the data. The three simultaneous equations may be solved by any convenient method for the three unknowns, a, b_1, and b_2.

To facilitate discussion of the three (or more) variable regression model, an actual computer output will be used. The output will serve to illustrate some of the additional statistics which are required for interpretation. A further benefit is the opportunity to study the format of the output of a commonly available computer regression program.

Illustrating Multiple Linear Regression Analysis

An example of a computer output for a four-variable, multiple regression forecasting analysis is shown in Figure 7–3. The printout is the result of a widely used regression program.[3] Other regression programs exist, and their output has a different appearance. The basic principles are the same, however.

The example used here is not held out as a good forecasting job. Rather, it is used because it illustrates a number of points which must be discussed concerning the use of regression analysis in forecasting. The model for the demand analysis of cocoa is that the quantity of cocoa demanded was influenced by price, personal income, and time.

For convenience the regression program allows the forecaster to assign a six-letter name to each of the variables. These may be actual words or any collection of six letters which will aid the forecaster in remembering which variable is which. In terms of the names used in Figure 7–3, the model may be stated as:

$$\text{DESGRI} = a + b_1 \text{ ISSTDI} + b_2 \text{ PERINC} + b_3 \text{ TIMERS} \quad (7\text{–}10)$$

The interpretation of this equation is the same as above. The job of the forecaster is to estimate a, b_1, b_2, and b_3.

---

[3] The particular output shown was generated by a BIMD 29 program on Northwestern University's CDC 6400 computer. The original source of the program was the Division of Biostatics, Dept. of Preventitive Medicine & Public Health, School of Medicine, UCLA.

FIGURE 7–3

```
PROBLEM NUMBER     2
REPLACEMENT AND DELETION   2

DEPENDENT VARIABLE IS NOW      8
NUMBER OF VARIABLES DELETED   22
VARIABLES DELETED...  1  2  3  5  6  7  9 11 12 13 14 15 16 17 18 19 20 24 25 26 27 28
```

ANALYSIS OF VARIANCE FOR REGRESSION				
SOURCE OF VARIATION	D.F.	SUM OF SQUARES	MEAN SQUARES	F VALUE
DUE TO REGRESSION.............	3	1443.78810	481.26270	90.40554
DEVIATION ABOUT REGRESSION...	35	186.31816	5.32338	
TOTAL...	38	1630.10627		

```
THE RESULTS ABOVE ARE ACCURATE TO NO MORE THAN SIX DECIMAL PLACES
DESPITE THE POSSIBLE ILLUSION OF GREATER ACCURACY
```

INTERCEPT (A VALUE) IS   38.82815

VARIABLE		MEAN	STANDARD DEVIATION	REG. COEF.	STD. ERROR OF REG.COEF.	COMPUTED T VALUE	PARTIAL CORR. COEF.
NO.	NAME						
21	ISSTDI	27.93333	7.94255	-.41735	.06212	-6.71866	-.75051
4	PERINC	421.18462	63.09754	.12027	.03648	3.29709	.48681
10	TIMERS	49.00000	11.40175	-.37467	.19576	-1.91398	-.30781
DEPENDENT							
8	DESGRI	59.46667	6.54962				

COMPARE CHECK ON FINAL COEFFICIENT.......   -.37467

INCREMENTS FOR INDEPENDENT VARIABLES				•	CUMULATIVE REGRESSIONS			
VARIABLE	SUMS OF SQUARES	PROP. VAR.	F VALUE EACH TERM	• STD. ERROR OF ESTIMATE	SUMS OF SQUARES	PROP.VAR. * R SQ.	F VALUE	MULTIPLE R
NO. NAME				•				
21 ISSTDI	1183.78808	.72620	98.13662	3.47313	1183.78808	.72620	98.13662	.85218
4 PERINC	240.49880	.14754	42.06580	2.39107	1424.28688	.87374	124.54166	.93474
10 TIMERS	19.50122	.01196	3.66332	2.30724	1443.78810	.88570	90.40554	.94112

```
PROPORTION OF VARIANCE SPE-
CIFIED TO LIMIT VARIABLES     .01000
```

The data for the regression analysis may be defined more precisely. The values recorded are on a quarterly basis. DESGRI refers to deseasonalized U.S. grindings of cocoa, a measure of usage. The explanatory or independent variables are: ISSTDI, the price of cocoa in Accra, lagged one quarter; PERINC, personal income in the U.S., seasonally adjusted quarterly at annual rates; and TIMERS, a variable for time formed by simple consecutive numbering of the quarters, starting with the first quarter of 1949. Using the data described, the regression analysis resulted in the sample output shown.

The numerical results of the regression analysis appear in the middle of the page. The computer value for a, designated the intercept value, stands alone. The estimates of the b_i are arrayed in a column headed regression coefficients. These results may be placed in the equation format as

$$\text{DESGRI} = 38.8 - 0.417 \text{ ISSTDI} + 0.12 \text{ PERINC} - 0.375 \text{ TIMERS} \quad (7\text{--}11)$$

A forecast of cocoa usage in thousands of long tons would be prepared by the substitution of appropriate values into the equation. For example, a forecast for quarter number 42 if the price were $.25 and personal income were expected to be $350 billion would be

DESGRI $= 38.8 - .417(.25) + .12(350)$
$$- .375(42) = 64{,}946 \text{ long tons}$$

Statistical Inference

Other statistics appear on the printout. These are very useful to the forecaster.[4] Each will be discussed in turn, from the top of the printout sheet.

F test.   The F value may be viewed in two ways. It may be thought of as a test that $b_1 = b_2 = b_3 = b_k = 0$. That is, all of the regression coefficients are the same and equal to zero, and there is no relationship at all. The other way of viewing the F test is a test that $R^2 = 0$. No reduction in variance results from the regression analysis.

The F value is a ratio defined as

$$F = \frac{R^2/k - 1}{1 - R^2/n - k - 1} \qquad (7\text{–}12)$$

In the present example, $F = 90.41$ as may be seen in the upper right of Figure 7–3. The number of variables in the model, including the dependent variable, is k, in this case 4. The number of observations is n, in the present example 38. The F value is meaningless in and of itself. The comparison value is found in the F tables. The value for $F_{3,35}$ is 4.40 at the 99 percent confidence level. Since 90.4 exceeds this substantially, it is possible to reject the null hypothesis that $R^2 = 0$ or that $b_i = 0$. Thus, there is a reduction in unexplained variance as a result of the

---

[4] The regression program may be used for other purposes than forecasting. Thus, other statistics not especially helpful to the forecaster appear. These are ignored.

regression analysis. It may be said that there exist a statistically significant relationship between the dependent and the independent variables.

t **values.** The next statistic to be considered is the *t* value. This statistic allows for a test of the statistical significance of each regression coefficient. The *t* ratio may be used to compare the regression coefficient with any number the forecaster has in mind. The most common null hypothesis is that $b_i = 0$. For this test, the *t* ratio is simply the ratio of the regression coefficient to the standard error of the regression coefficient. Both of these numbers and the *t* ratio appear in the printout. The *t* ratio associated with b_1 is seen to be $t_1 = -.41735/.06212 = -6.71866$. This number in itself means nothing. However, tables of values of *t* ratios exist, and with these it is possible to make the appropriate tests.

Referring to the *t* tables, one may see that, for the sample size in the cocoa example, the 99 percent confidence value for *t* is 3.59 and the 95 percent confidence value is 2.996. From these values, it is easy to see why some people who work with regression analysis adopt the "eyeball" *t* test of insisting that the regression coefficient be at least twice its standard error. In the cocoa example, without regard to the sign, a *t* value of 6.7 means that $b_1 = .417$ differs from zero at better than the 99 percent confidence level while $b_2 = .120$ differs from zero with 95 percent confidence. However, with a *t* value of 1.91, $b_3 = 0.375$ could not be said to differ significantly from zero at the 95 percent level of confidence, a commonly used cut-off level in statistical work. Thus, while the time trend seems to reduce the unexplained variance, in fact the forecaster may not have gained anything at all by the inclusion of this variable.

Partial Correlation Coefficient. The partial correlation coefficients are precisely the same as the correlation coefficient in the two-variable case. Only in multiple regression is an additional feature added. The value given for each variable is the amount of the variance of the dependent variable explained by the independent variable, given that the value of the other independent variables in the model are held statistically constant. In the example above, the correlation between the variation in quantity of cocoa used and its price is $-.75$ after the variation due to changes in income and the time trend have been removed by the statistical technique.

Multiple Coefficient of Determination. The multiple coefficient of determination is exactly analogous to the simple coefficient of determination, except that the amount of "explained" variation is that contributed by the several independent variables. Both R and R^2 appear to the lower right of the printout page. Formally, R^2 is

$$R^2 = \frac{\Sigma(\hat{q} - \bar{\hat{q}})^2}{\Sigma(q - \bar{q})^2} \qquad (7\text{--}13)$$

In words, it is the ratio of the sum of squared deviations of the forecast values from the mean of the forecast values to the sum of the squared deviations of the observed values from the mean of the values. Of course, $\bar{\hat{q}} = \bar{q}$, since the procedure forces the regression hyperplane through the mean of the observed values. Thus, if the $\hat{q}$ or forecasts were exactly the same as the observed q, the ratio would be unity.

In the present example the proportion of variance explained (R^2) by the price variable is 73 percent. Adding personal income explains an additional 15 percent for a total of 87 percent, while the time trend boosts the explained proportion to 88.6 percent. Remember, this last increase is illusory, since the coefficient for the time variable is not statistically significant.

Durbin-Watson Statistic. Two more statistics computed by the BIMD 29 regression program, are worthy of note by the forecaster. These usually appear on a separate page of the computer printout. This page for the cocoa example appears below in Figure 7–4. Both of these statistics are designed to test for serial correlation or autocorrelation in the data. Autocorrelation means that the assumption of independence has been violated and that one observation or data point tends to be correlated with the next. This is a problem for forecasters, as they frequently work with time-series data, and time series are frequently autocorrelated. Methods for dealing with autocorrelation are discussed in the next chapter. The next few paragraphs simply cover the tests for its presence.

The first of the two statistics is the Durbin-Watson statistic. It is computed by

$$d = \frac{\sum_{t=2}^{n} [(q - \hat{q})_t - (q - \hat{q})_{t-1}]^2}{\sum_{t=1}^{n} (q - \hat{q})_t^2} \qquad (7\text{–}14)$$

In the example given, $d = .87394$. A precise test of this statistic is made difficult by the necessity to refer to the original articles in *Biometrika,* 1950 and 1951, by Durbin and Watson in order to find appropriate tables. Once the tables have been located, the forecaster learns not one but two values for his sample size (n) and number of explanatory variables. If his computed d is less than the smaller of the two numbers, he has positive autocorrelation, as in the example given. If his computed d is larger than the larger number from the tables, he is sure that there is no autocorrelation. However, if the computed d falls between the two values, the test is inconclusive and the forecaster is not sure about autocorrelation.

von Neumann Ratio. The von Neumann ratio is more commonly used in analysis of residuals for autocorrelation. Another name for this statistic is ratio of the mean-square successive difference to the variance. It is defined as

$$\frac{\dfrac{\displaystyle\sum_{t=2}^{n}[(q-\hat{q})_{t+1}-(q-\hat{q})_t]^2}{n-1}}{\dfrac{\displaystyle\sum_{t=1}^{n}(q-\hat{q})^2}{n}} \qquad (7\text{-}15)$$

In Figure 7–4, it may be seen that the von Neumann ratio is .89694. For a sample size of 38, ratios smaller than 1.31 would occur 1 percent of the time in random drawings from a non-autocorrelated population. Since the computed ratio is less than 1.31, the forecaster must conclude that there is strong positive autocorrelation, a confirmation of the Durbin-Watson result.

FIGURE 7–4

VON NEUMANN RATIO	.89694
DURBIN-WATSON COEFFICIENT	.87394

RANGE OF RESIDUALS.................	9.404
RANGE / STD. ERROR OF ESTIMATE....	4.076

Some econometricians currently favor the von Neumann ratio over the Durbin-Watson statistic, though in the present example both gave the same result. There is a further question as to whether autocorrelation is a problem for the forecaster. In many cases, to the extent that it does exist, simple transformations of the data will enable the forecaster to deal with it. These transformations, along with a variety of other regression techniques, will be left to the next chapter.

PROBLEMS

1. In Table 1 are data on price and quantity sold of widgets.

   a) Using regression analysis, estimate the demand function.

   b) The sales personnel report that widgets are currently selling between $0.46 and $0.48. Prepare a forecast for the production people to use in planning future production.

TABLE 1

Sales of Widgets—Number and Average Price
(per 2 month reporting period)

Sales (000)	Price	Sales (000)	Price
557	19.0¢	570	18.8
495	54.6	514	40.9
490	60.6	568	30.6
512	50.9	567	25.0
530	43.6	595	28.7
552	32.9	562	27.6
568	17.2	483	64.7¢

2. Table 2 contains data on quarterly sales of a fertilizer in tons, the price per ton and the amount of advertising purchased in magazines directed at the farm population.

TABLE 2

Fertilizer Sales, Price and Expenditures for Advertising

Sales (1,000 tons)	Price per Ton	Advertising (000 omitted)
200.3	$73.10	$ 9.6
202.5	73.10	11.0
128.7	53.10	7.5
122.5	42.10	5.4
214.7	81.60	11.8
137.0	60.70	6.8
180.1	72.90	10.1
156.8	65.80	7.3
117.1	38.80	5.5
206.7	$73.70	$11.0

a) Use regression analysis to fit the demand equation. (Price-quantity only.)

b) Now fit the three-variable case which accounts for variation in advertising expenditures. Compare your results with part *a*.

c) Because of the competitive nature of agriculture it is difficult to determine what the selling price will be, but the marketing department feels that the price will average near $75.00 per ton if present conditions hold. Planned advertising expenditures are $10,000. Prepare a forecast of fertilizer sales. If you do the regressions on a computer, prepare high and low forecasts as well.

REFERENCES

BRENNAN, MICHAEL J. *Preface to Econometrics.* 2d ed. Cincinnati: Southwestern Publishing Company, 1965.

EZEKIAL, MORDECAI, and KARL A. FOX. *Methods of Correlation and Regression Analysis.* 3d ed. New York: John Wiley & Sons, Inc., 1959.

JOHNSTON, J. *Econometric Methods.* New York: McGraw-Hill Book Company, Inc., 1963.

KLEIN, L. R. *An Introduction to Econometrics.* Englewood Cliffs, N.J.: Prentice-Hall, Inc., 1962.

TINTNER, GERHARD. *Econometrics.* New York: John Wiley & Sons, Inc., 1952.

chapter
—8—
Additional Regression Problems and Techniques

The last chapter dealt with regression analysis per se. But in many respects the regression is the least part of the forecaster's job. The more difficult operations very quickly carry the forecaster into the field of econometrics, which is by no means an elementary subject. Thus, the pattern begun in the discussion of regression will be continued—i.e. a heuristic rather than a formal approach is in order. The intention here is not to treat the subject matter of econometrics but rather to touch upon a number of problem areas and some suggested techniques for working in these areas.

At this level problems of model building interact with regression analysis. In this chapter the fitting of nonlinear relationships, the use of data transformations to eliminate autocorrelation, and models of adjustment with a lag will be considered. The question of simultaneous determination of results will be discussed in the context of a supply and demand model. This model also illustrates a number of considerations such as identification, multicolinearity, and estimation by two-stage least-squares regression. Finally, multiequation models will be discussed.

The material in this chapter is substantially more difficult than that which has preceded. More than casual effort is required for understanding. Some readers will wish to skip this chapter until they have some need for the contents.

Nonlinear Relationships

It was stated in the preceding chapter that plotting the data would often be useful to the forecaster. In particular, such a plot may reveal the relationship between the variables to be other than a straight line. If so, a better "fit" of the data will be obtained if a nonlinear function is used. A large number of nonlinear mathematical functions could be estimated by linear regression methods. Two such relationships are considered here.

The mathematical forms discussed here were chosen for two reasons. First, they are relatively simple. Second, many regression programs have built into them the necessary transformations of the data required to fit such functions by linear regression. The log-linear function has the additional desirable property that the coefficients estimated have an economic interpretation.

Parabola. A function which may be fitted to many nonlinear relationships is the parabola. The letter Y is used to represent the dependent variable and X to represent the independent variable, and the function to be estimated is

$$Y = a + b_1 X + b_2 X^2 \qquad (8\text{--}1)$$

which is the general form of a parabola and the same as the three-variable regression model discussed above.

If the plot of the data reveals a nonlinear relationship, the forecaster may well want to consider fitting this form. The parabola is easy to use because the basic computer program does some of the work. The forecaster feeds in the data on Y and X. For convenience X may be renamed X_1 and the computer asked to generate $X_2 = X_1^2$. The regression is then run as which is the same as Equation (8–1) above.

$$Y = a + b_1 X_1 + b_2 X_2 \qquad (8\text{–}2)$$

In Figure 8–1 a hypothetical plotting of data reveals a nonlinear relationship. If Y and X are considered to be price and quantity, then the function to be obtained is the usual demand curve of economic analysis. If the data plotted in Figure 8–1 were used to estimate Equation (8–2), the parabola shown in Figure 8–1 would result.

Of course, the forecaster is interested only in the portion of the parabola which is shown as a solid line in Figure 8–1, for

FIGURE 8–1

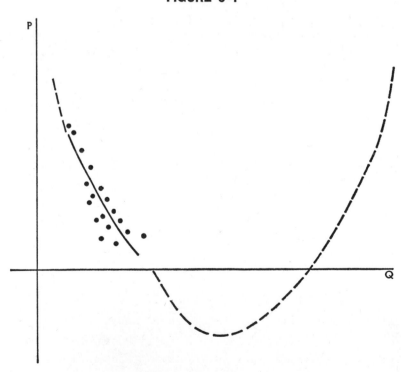

that is where the data points are. The regression procedure will produce from the data an equation which represents the entire parabola, but the forecasts will be in or near the range represented by the solid line.

The forecaster is not limited to two variables in the nonlinear case. Relationships may be nonlinear in several dimensions. It may even be necessary to combine linear and nonlinear relationships. For example, the model may be that a particular variable is linearly related to two variables but has a nonlinear relationship with a third. The equation to be fit becomes

$$Y = a + b_1 X_1 + b_2 X_1^2 + b_3 X_2 + b_4 X_3 \qquad (8\text{--}3)$$

Another possibility is to seek higher powers of the variable which yield curves more closely fitting the observed data. Thus, a curve like

$$Y = a + b_1 X + b_2 X^2 + b_3 X^3 \qquad (8\text{--}4)$$

would be fit. There is no limit to the exponents which might be used except, of course, the number of data points available. It is possible that a curve will be found which exactly passes through all the data points but which is of no use in predicting the next observation.

Log-Linear.   The forecaster may also want to consider functions like

$$q = \alpha p^{\beta_1} y^{\beta_2} \qquad (8\text{--}5)$$

This demand function is nonlinear in both price and income. By taking logs of this function the forecaster obtains the equation:

$$ln\ q = ln\ \alpha + \beta_1\ ln\ p + \beta_2\ ln\ y \qquad (8\text{--}6)$$

The log form of this relationship is linear and may be fit in the usual way. The log transformation is made easy for the forecaster, since the regression program also has this feature built in. There is no need to look up the logs of the numbers. The regression program in many instances will perform the transformation and compute the regression coefficients on the transformed variables.

Additional variables are easily added to the analysis. For example, if the forecaster felt that the price of a close substitute influenced sales of the product in question, the model becomes

$$q = \alpha p^{\beta_1} y^{\beta_2} p_s^{\beta_3} \tag{8-7}$$

where p_s is the price of the substitute. The regression becomes

$$ln\ q = ln\ \alpha + \beta_1\ ln\ p + \beta_2\ ln\ y + \beta_3\ ln\ p_s \tag{8-8}$$

Additional variables may be added if data are available.

The above function is a hyperbola when plotted on an arithmetic scale. It has the convenient property that it is a constant elasticity function. The coefficients are estimates of own-price elasticity (β_1), income elasticity (β_2) and cross-price elasticity (β_3). The equation defining elasticity is

$$\eta = \frac{\dfrac{\Delta q}{q}}{\dfrac{\Delta p}{p}} \tag{8-9}$$

That is, elasticity is defined as the percentage change in quantity divided by the percentage change in price. But it is the nature of logarithms that changes are percentage changes; hence

$$\eta = \frac{\Delta ln\ q}{\Delta ln\ p} = \beta_1 \tag{8-10}$$

The regression coefficient is the elasticity estimated at the geometric mean of the data points. The curve fit in this fashion will have the same elasticity everywhere. Since this may not in fact be true, the forecaster must recognize the peril of using a curve to forecast far beyond the domain of the data points. This warning must be especially emphasized in situations where logarithmic data are used, because both the logs and the associated errors get very large quickly as one moves upward on the scale.

Time-Series Problems

One common form of data which forecasters use is time series—that is, observations on a variable at a number of points in time. However, there is a potential difficulty with time series. The present section explores the nature of the difficulty and proposes a means of overcoming it.

Consider the hypothetical time series illustrated in Figure 8–2. The variable Y could be any forecast variable. The straight line is a regression line with respect to time (and perhaps some other variables). The difficulty is immediately obvious. For time periods three through five, the $(\hat{Y} - Y)$ are all positive, while for periods seven through ten $(\hat{Y} - Y) < 0$ holds. This condition is called autocorrelation of the residuals. Such a condition arises frequently with time series.

Autocorrelation violates the conditions required to produce a valid regression estimate. To be strictly correct, each observation on the data should be totally independent of any other observation. Time series do not meet this condition. Almost any observation in the series may be forecast by the last observation plus or minus a small change. This is especially true where a strong trend exists, such as in Figure 8–1. The important point is that the change from one observation to the next is small and predictable. In effect, each entry in the time series is much the same—that is, highly correlated with the entries on either side. As a result, the differences between the trend line and the observations tend to exhibit patterns which produce the result noted in Figure 8–2.

Remember that one of the assumptions of regression analysis is that the errors about the regression line are small and unrelated to each other and that the expected value is zero.[1] Clearly, this assumption is violated. If one of the residuals is known to be greater than zero, then it is probable that the next is greater than zero also, over several successive observations.

Of course, the regression program does not recognize the presence of autocorrelation. It will produce regression coefficients in the usual manner. But the forecaster needs to be aware, through observation of a plot of the residuals or a test

FIGURE 8–2

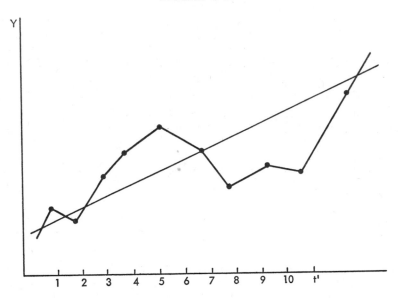

of the von Neumann ratio, that autocorrelation exists. If there is autocorrelation, the least-squares regression procedure may give serious underestimates of the true variance. This will lead to rejection of the null hypothesis that the $b_i = 0$ based on the t and F tests, when in fact it should not have been rejected. Similarly, confidence intervals will be set much too narrow. Thus, the forecaster may be misled.

---

[1] See Chapter 7.

Is it possible to save the regression analysis when autocorrelation exists? Procedures do exist which enable the forecaster to say something about the nature of the autocorrelation and use this knowledge to improve the efficiency (in the statistical sense) of his estimates. Two schemes are considered here: use of first differences and direct estimation of the autocorrelation coefficient.

First Differences. If forecasting the level of a variable poses difficulties, perhaps it is possible to forecast changes in the variable. If the changes in the level of the forecast variable are the result of changes in other variables, then it makes sense to obtain such forecasts directly. Further, it turns out that many economic time series which contain autocorrelation in the residuals when the raw data are used exhibit no autocorrelation of residuals from a regression in which first differences are used.

The regression equation becomes

$$Y_t - Y_{t-1} = a + \sum_i b_i (X_{it} - X_{it-1}) \qquad (8\text{--}11)$$

This is a convenient form to fit, since many regression programs contain a built-in routine to take the first differences. Of course, the forecaster ends up with fewer observations, since one is lost in the process. But substantial gains may be made. Referring to the hypothetical time series in Figure 8–2 above, notice that in time periods seven through ten there are more changes in sign of the differences than in the level of the variable. Thus, residuals from the regression of first differences should not be autocorrelated, and the forecaster may prepare a forecast of changes in the variable with a greater degree of confidence.

Autoregressive Regression. A more direct approach to serial correlation problems is to estimate directly the autocorrelation coefficient. The use of first differences implies an autoregressive scheme in which the coefficient of autocorrelation is unity. If some other value is more correct, it should be estimated and used. The estimation equation is

$$Y_t - \hat{Y}_t = \alpha(Y_{t-1} - \hat{Y}_{t-1}) + e_t \qquad (8\text{–}12)$$

Since $E(e_t) = 0$ and the e_t are not autocorrelated, α is estimated by

$$\alpha = \frac{\displaystyle\sum_{t=2}^{n}(Y_t - \hat{Y}_t)(Y_{t-1} - \hat{Y}_{t-1})}{\displaystyle\sum_{t=2}^{n}(Y_{t-1} - \hat{Y}_{t-1})} \qquad (8\text{–}13)$$

The regression equation now becomes

$$(Y_t - \alpha\hat{Y}_{t-1}) = a + \sum_i b_i(X_{it} - \alpha X_{it-1}) \qquad (8\text{–}14)$$

which should be compared with Equation (8–11) above. For $\alpha = 1$, they are identical. Because the α's are computed from the $(Y - \hat{Y})$'s, which may be written $Y - a - \sum_i b_i X_i$, it is appropriate to use the same α to transform all the variables.

Figure 8–3 shows the table of residuals generated by the regression program for the cocoa regression in the last chapter. The column of residuals $(Y - \hat{Y})$ may be used in equation (8–13) to compute the autoregressive coefficient. The result is $\alpha = .599$. The same α value is used to transform each observation because, as is stated in the paragraph above, all of the observations were used in computing α.

From the data in Figure 8–2, it may be seen that $Y_{39} = 73.66$ and $Y_{38} = 72.16$, so that transformation becomes

$$\begin{aligned} Y'_{39} &= 73.66 - .559(72.16) \\ &= 33.32 \end{aligned}$$

This process is repeated for each of the observations on Y and all of the X's as well—except the dummy variable TIMERS, for which the transformation may be meaningless. The regression equation becomes

$$\text{DESGRI}_t - .559 \text{ DESGRI}_{t-1} = a(1 - .559) + b_1(\text{ISSTDI}_t$$
$$- .559 \text{ ISSTDI}_{t-1}) + b_2(\text{PERINC}_t - .559 \text{ PERINC}_{t-1})$$
$$+ b_3'\text{TIMERS}$$
$$(8\text{--}15)$$

which would give estimates of the regression coefficients for which confidence intervals could be calculated free of any bias introduced by the presence of autocorrelation.

FIGURE 8-3

Table of Residuals

OBSERVATION	DESGRI Y VALUE	Y ESTIMATE	Y - Ŷ RESIDUAL
1	56.45000	55.12624	1.32376
2	54.61000	56.12747	-1.51747
3	58.24000	56.07618	2.16382
4	57.38000	57.95312	-.57312
5	59.69000	58.14936	1.54064
6	55.91000	56.60478	-.69478
7	58.43000	54.38740	4.04260
8	53.55000	52.53999	1.01001
9	50.60000	48.45874	2.14126
10	51.79000	47.89605	3.89395
11	50.35000	49.08899	1.26101
12	51.82000	53.12061	-1.30061
13	51.54000	53.09974	-1.55974
14	48.21000	52.60059	-4.39059
15	50.07000	53.72774	-3.65774
16	54.31000	56.68700	-2.37700
17	51.85000	57.21147	-5.36147
18	52.44000	57.28600	-4.84600
19	56.38000	57.20347	-.82347
20	57.28000	58.60293	-1.32293
21	59.27000	60.06468	-.79468
22	61.87000	60.39466	1.47534
23	62.89000	61.72205	1.16795
24	60.83000	61.76482	-.93482
25	63.56000	62.34521	1.21479
26	63.49000	62.47566	1.01434
27	63.07000	63.57311	-.50311
28	66.48000	64.50505	1.97495
29	64.40000	62.14345	2.25655
30	65.55000	61.59063	3.95937
31	64.09000	63.13800	.95200
32	64.75000	64.08341	.66659
33	64.61000	64.04487	.56513
34	66.85000	65.67006	1.17994
35	66.14000	66.16132	-.02132
36	66.57000	67.80070	-1.23070
37	68.06000	69.17342	-1.11342
38	72.16000	72.62938	-.46938
39	73.66000	73.97167	-.31167

$$\alpha = \frac{\sum\limits_{t=2}^{n} (Y_t - \hat{Y}_t)(Y_{t-1} - \hat{Y}_{t-1})}{\sum\limits_{t=2}^{n}(Y_{t-1} - \hat{Y}_{t-1})^2}$$

$$= .559$$

Lagged Variables

The forecaster may find that he knows fairly well the variables which will influence the one he is trying to forecast but that, from either economic theory or practical experience, he also knows that there is a time lag. For example, in many macroeconomic models the consumption function is specified

$$C_t = a + b\, y_{t-1}$$

as which says that consumption this month (quarter, year) is a function of income last month (quarter, year).

Time lags are not uncommon. People do not always change behavior patterns immediately. There may be economic reasons as well. Commitments of one type or another run for long periods of time. Existing stocks of goods or existing investments will delay response. When the forecaster feels that such lags exist, he need only alter his regression analysis to the extent that the observations match the current value of the forecast variable with earlier values of the independent variables.

Once estimated, such a model has obvious advantages for the forecaster. His regression analysis gives him the response of the variable which he is forecasting to the level of another variable(s) in earlier periods. When data representing the independent variables for the present period are used, the calculation obviously yields an estimate of the forecast variable in period $t + 1$, the period to be forecast. Successive solutions of the equation yield forecasts as many periods in the future as desired.

The danger with lagged variables is that it is possible (inadvertently?) let the same variable appear on both sides of the equal sign. No competent forecaster would regress a variable on itself. But it almost sounds plausible to suggest that market share this quarter depends on market share last quarter plus some other things. Since this introduces obvious serial correlation, the results of such a regression analysis would be at best misleading and more likely of no use whatsoever.

A logical extension of a one-period lag model would be one incorporating distributed lags. A distributed-lags model would be used if the adjustment process is not complete within one period. It is also used when expectations of the future determine behavior and hence the variable to be forecast. The underlying assumption, for want of a better one, is that expectations of the future are formed on the basis of past experience, with more recent periods having the greatest impact on expectations. The equation estimated might take the form

$$Y = a + b_1 \sum_{i=1}^{n} w_i X_{1i} + b_2 \sum_{j=1}^{m} w_j X_{2j} \qquad (8\text{--}17)$$

The weights, *w*, and the number of periods to include are in turn determined by a series of regression solutions. The weights assigned to more distant past time periods are smaller than the weights for more recent periods. A detailed description of the estimation of the weights is beyond the scope of this chapter.[2] The use of the equation estimated for forecasting purposes is the same as above.

Dummy Variables

Another helpful technique for the forecaster using regression analysis is the zero-one or dummy variable. One or more such dummy variables may be employed in a regression analysis when the forecaster feels that there has been a sharp shift in the function he is trying to estimate.

As has been mentioned, it is important that the forecaster plot his data and visually examine the pattern obtained. Suppose the forecaster obtained a plot such as is shown in Figure 8–4. Inspection reveals two clusters of points which seem to lie along roughly similarly sloped lines. This observation would be reinforced if each of the points plotted were dated and there were dates from one period in one cluster and from another period in the other cluster.

The model would take the form

$$Y = a + b_1 X + b_2 D$$

---

[2] A good reference on this topic, now becoming difficult to obtain, is Nerlove, M., *Distributed Lags and Demand Analysis for Agriculture and Other Commodities*, U.S. Dept. of Agriculture, Agricultural Handbook 141.

For each of the $X:Y$ pairs in the upper cluster, D would take on the value of one. Similarly, for each of the $X:Y$ pairs in the lower cluster, D would have the value of zero. The assignment of zero-one is arbitrary and could easily be reversed. This technique would in effect allow estimation of the $X:Y$ relationship from all of the data available and at the same time take out the influence of the shift in the relationship which obviously exists.

FIGURE 8–4

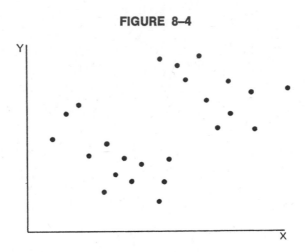

The matter of a parallel shift in the schedule requires further comment. To be absolutely correct, either economic theory or visual inspection should indicate that the shift in the curve does not affect the slope of the curve before the dummy variable is used. Thus, using zero-one dummy variables to differentiate before and after the 10 percent surcharge on the federal income tax is incorrect, since the surcharge is known to change the slope. In practice the rule is often violated, though not without some attendant jeopardy to the forecaster.

Another common violation of a strict interpretation is the use of dummy variables to account for shifts in nonquantifiable variables. For example, a change in political parties may be thought to influence the variable to be forecast in a subtle way

Including dummy variables in the model may allow the forecaster to account for some of the influence.

While the term "dummy variable" is usually reserved for a zero-one dummy, there is no strict reason for its being so. In the cocoa model discussed above, the passage of time was represented by a simple numbering of the time periods for which the data were collected. The use of this type of dummy allows the forecaster to remove any trends and to account for a variety of subtle shifts over time which he cannot quantify and build explicitly into the model.

Simultaneous Systems of Equations

The forecaster will frequently find that two or more variables which he plans to forecast are simultaneously determined. In order to forecast in such a situation, he must have a model which will enable him to sort out the various influences, and he needs a means of estimating the separate equations involved. The simplest example of a system of the sort described would be the usual supply and demand analysis. Two equations, supply and demand, representing separate sets of economic forces, are solved simultaneously for price and quantity. The forecaster needs to know something about both equations to make an accurate forecast.

When simultaneous systems are used, some additional problems are presented to the forecaster. For purposes of illustrating those problems and the means of coping with them, it will be useful to develop another example. While not originally intended as a forecasting model, it would certainly be useful for such purposes. The model represents the market for farmland as influenced by technological advances.[3] If desired, forecasts of farmland prices could be derived.

---

[3] Herdt, R. W., and W. W. Cochrane, "Farm Land Prices and Farm Technological Advance," *Journal of Farm Economics,* Vol. 48. no. 2, May, 1966, pp. 243–63.

In the market for farmland the supply equation was thought to be

$$S = S(P,R,U,LF)$$

where S = number of farms per thousand farms supplied, P = average price per acre of land and buildings in current dollars, R = interest on high grade bonds, Standard & Poor, U = unemployment ratio, and LF = land in farms. The demand equation is specified as

$$D = D(P,R,T,P_r/P_p, UL, WPI) \qquad (8\text{--}19)$$

where D = number of farms per thousand demanded, P and R the same as above, T = USDA index of productivity, P_r/P_p = ratio of index of prices received by farmers to index of prices paid by farmers (parity ratio), UL = urban land, and WPI = Wholesale Price Index. A third equation,

$$S = D \qquad (8\text{--}20)$$

was included to assure market clearance, but it is not an independent equation. Thus, the model is two Equations, (8–18) and (8–19), and two unknowns, P and $S = D$.

For completeness, it should be pointed out that several of the variables were lagged according to the formula

$$X_t = \frac{3X_{t-1} + 2X_{t-2} + X_{t-3}}{6} \qquad (8\text{--}21)$$

In terms of the notation of distributed lags, the w_1 was $3/6 = .5$, $w_2 = .33$ and $w_3 = .167$. The notation X refers to the variables which were lagged by Equation (8–21). The variables lagged were T, P_r/P_p and WPI. The reasons for choosing Equation (8–21) to lag the data were not revealed by the authors, though by inference a better fit was obtained from the use of the data lagged in this manner rather than from the raw data.

Since both price and quantity appear in both equations, the

choice of which is the dependent in each is arbitrary. If quantity is chosen to be dependent in the supply equation, the equations to be estimated may be written as

$$S = a + b_1 P + b_2 R + b_3 U + b_4 LF \qquad (8\text{-}22)$$

$$P = c + d_1 D + d_2 R + d_3 T$$
$$+ d_4 P_r/P_p + d_5 UL + d_6 WPI \quad (8\text{-}23)$$

$$S = D \qquad (8\text{-}24)$$

which is the linear system of equations to be estimated. The forecaster might estimate these equations by linear regression, using yearly data from 1910 to 1962, as the authors of the study did. The most immediate difficulty is that this system of equations is over-identified. What this means and why it is a problem must be explained.

Identification. The subject of identification does not lend itself to a simple treatment. Nevertheless, the idea of identification can be illustrated in a fairly direct manner. Formal statements of identification rules will be given. For detailed discussion of the statements the reader is referred to the references at the end of Chapter 7.

The question of identification ultimately comes down to the ability to estimate the desired equation or equations from the data. For example, supposing the forecaster had observed the price-quantity combinations shown in Figure 8–5. It is possible to fit a regression line to these data points, but it is not clear that either a demand or a supply equation would be the result. Each of the points represents an intersection of the supply and demand equations, but both curves may have jumped around. One such pair is illustrated. The trick is to find the variables which caused the curves to move around. Hopefully, it will be possible to find variables which shift demand but not supply and vice versa.

Suppose the demand function was specified by

$$Q_D = a + b_1 P + b_2 X \qquad (8\text{-}25)$$

where X is some variable which influences demand but not supply. Assume that X is the only variable which causes the demand schedule to shift. If the forecaster knows nothing more about the supply function, then the introduction of X into the demand function allows him, in effect, to hold the demand

FIGURE 8–5

curve steady while the movements of the supply function trace out the shape of the demand curve. But the system of both supply and demand equations remains under-identified, in that it is still impossible to estimate the supply curve.

Now, suppose a variable which affects supply but not demand and which accounts for all the movement in the supply curve is introduced into the model. The equation becomes

$$Q_s = c + d_1 P + d_2 Y \qquad (8\text{--}26)$$

Since it is now possible to explain the movements of both the supply and the demand equation, it is also possible to estimate all the parameters of the system. Such a system is termed just-identified.

There is yet one more step. Now suppose that there are two

variables which taken together are thought to account for the movement in the supply equation but which have no impact on the demand equation. The supply equation then becomes

$$Q_S = c + d_1 P + d_2 Y + d_3 Z \qquad (8\text{-}27)$$

The system is now over-identified. It is no longer possible to obtain unique estimates of d_2 and d_3 by ordinary least-squares regressions. The techniques for estimating over-identified systems will be discussed below. Before we turn to that topic, a more formal statement of the identification criteria may now be made.

In the formal manner one must adopt the habit of mathematics and speak of necessary and sufficient conditions. The conditions apply to the behavioral equations of a model such as Equations (8-25) and (8-26) or (8-27) of the present model. An equation such as $Q_S = Q_D$ is an identity, and, while it may be a part of the system, it does not help in identifying the system.

The necessary condition for identification is that the number of variables not contained in a particular equation but appearing elsewhere in the model must be one less than the number of endogenous or dependent variables. This statement may be made must less formidable by means of an illustration.

Consider the model as specified by Equations (8-25) and (8-26), repeated here for convenience.

$$Q_D = a + b_1 P + b_2 X \qquad (8\text{-}25)$$

$$Q_S = c + d_1 P + d_2 Y \qquad (8\text{-}26)$$

There are two endogenous or dependent variables, Q_S or Q_D and P. Thus, it must be possible to find one variable excluded from each equation but contained elsewhere in the model. In the demand equation, Y does not appear but is in the model. The demand equation is then identified. Similarly, the supply equation is identified, because X is excluded but appears elsewhere.

To perceive under-identification, suppose the model were:

$$Q_D = a + b_1 P + b_2 X \qquad (8\text{--}25)$$

$$Q_S = c + d_1 P \qquad (8\text{--}28)$$
$$Q_S = Q_D$$

The supply equation is identified, since X is excluded but contained in the model. But the demand equation is not identified, for there is no variable which meets the necessary condition. Since one equation is not identified, the system is not identified and may not be estimated. Intuition fails at this point. The reverse seems true. The reason the supply equation is identified is that the existence of X in the demand equation enables the forecaster to account for some of the movements of the demand equation and thus trace out the supply equation. If this were a mathematical discussion, it could be shown that it is the knowledge of b_2 that enables the forecaster to obtain estimates of c and d_1.

Finally, over-identification, as before, would occur when the model is

$$Q_D = a + b_1 P + b_2 X \qquad (8\text{--}25)$$

$$Q_S = c + d_1 P + d_2 Y + d_3 Z \qquad (8\text{--}27)$$
$$Q_S = Q_D$$

Again, the supply curve is identified but the demand curve is over-identified, because there are two variables, Y and Z, which are excluded but appear elsewhere.

The necessary and sufficient condition for identification is more complex and requires some knowledge of linear algebra—it must be possible to form, from the coefficients of the variables excluded from any given equation but contained in the other behavioral equations, one nonvanishing determinant equal to one less than the number of endogenous variables. While this statement seems confusing, it is simply saying that in the just-identified system of Equations (8–25) and (8–26), b_2 and d_2 must not be equal to zero.

In Equations (8–22) and (8–23), it is now obvious that the system is over-identified. By the necessary condition, one variable should be excluded from each but contained in the other. The quantity equation has four; $T, P_r / P_p$, UL, and WPI, while the price equation has two, U and LF.

The reader may be wondering just what the problem really is. Why not simply run the regressions as stated on Equations (8–22) and (8–23)? After all, these are perfectly good linear equations, and the technique of linear regressions may certainly be applied. The answer is that, in a system of jointly determined variables, the results of such regressions may be shown to be both biased and inconsistent. The reader will be spared a formal proof of these contentions, but it is necessary to explain what the terms mean.

There are four characteristics of an estimator or a statistic which statisticians are concerned about. A good statistic is

1. Unbiased—The statistical estimate converges on the true value for the population with repeated sampling and samples of the same size.
2. Consistent—The statistical estimate converges on the true value for the population as the sample size grows.
3. Efficient—The statistic exhibits the smallest variance among all possible estimators.
4. Sufficient—The statistic contains all the information available in the given sample.

In most econometric work it is not possible to find a statistic which embodies all of these characteristics. The econometrician or forecaster may have to make some trades, such as using a statistic which is less efficient in order to achieve a lower bias.

In the present case it may be shown that in a simultaneous system, direct estimates of the coefficients will always be biased and inconsistent, regardless of sample size. The results of direct estimates by regression would always be incorrect. Thus, the forecaster needs a means of avoiding errors of this type. Fortunately, techniques do exist. Some additional terms are required and will be developed in the context of the just-identified model.

$$Q_D = a + b_1 P + b_2 X \qquad (8\text{--}25)$$

$$Q_S = c + d_1 P + d_2 Y \qquad (8\text{--}26)$$

$$Q_S = Q_D \qquad (8\text{--}29)$$

These are referred to as the structural equations and, for the reasons given just above, may not be estimated directly. But it is possible to estimate indirectly the coefficients. For convenience, since $Q_S = Q_D$, replace both with Z. Then solve the system for P and Z. The result is

$$P = \frac{c - a}{b_1 - d_1} + \frac{d_2}{b_1 - d_1} Y - \frac{b_2}{b_1 - d_1} X \qquad (8\text{--}30)$$

$$Z = \frac{ad_1 - b_1 c}{d_1 - b_1} - \frac{b_1 d_2}{d_1 - b_1} Y + \frac{d_1 b_2}{d_1 - b_1} X \qquad (8\text{--}31)$$

Equations (8–30) and (8–31) are referred to as the reduced-form equations. These are not new equations but devices which the forecaster has constructed in order to estimate the parameters of the system of structural equations. The reduced-form equations may be estimated by ordinary least-squares regression. Six estimated parameters will be obtained from the reduced-form equations. The result is

$$e_1 = \frac{c - a}{b_1 - d_1} \qquad e_2 = \frac{d_2}{b_1 - d_1} \qquad e_3 = \frac{b_2}{b_1 - d_1}$$

$$e_4 = \frac{ad_1 - b_1 c}{d_1 - b_1} \qquad e_5 = \frac{b_1 d_2}{d_1 - b_1} \qquad e_6 = \frac{d_1 b_2}{d_1 - b_1}$$

The e_i are the results of the regression run on Equations (8–30) and (8–31). Thus, there is a system of six equations in six unknowns which may be solved for a, b_1, b_2, c, d_1, and d_2, the parameters of the structural Equations (8–25) and (8–26).

Is this circuitous route worth the effort? While the answer in practice is sometimes no, in theory it is yes. The estimates obtained in this manner may be shown to be consistent. However, they remain biased as before, though the bias is smaller. The formal proofs of these statements, are available in most econometrics texts.

The reader may already suspect that there is a reason why the just-identified model was used in the above discussion. The answer is fairly simple. In an under-identified system the e_i are fewer than the number of parameters in the structural equations. Thus, there is no solution obtainable.

On the other hand, in an over-identified system there are more e_i than parameters. Thus, depending on the order in which the equations are solved, there may be one or more estimates of the value of the parameters of the structural equation, none of which may be correct.

Since it is obvious that the discussion cannot end here, the alert reader will have already figured out that there is at least one technique which the forecaster may use to solve over-identified systems. Indeed, there are quite a few. There are (1) full information, maximum likelihood; (2) limited information, maximum likelihood; (3) three-stage least-squares; (4) two-stage least-squares, and (5) instrumental variables. All of the methods are biased but consistent. The methods are listed approximately in decreasing order of both efficiency (i.e., increasing variance of estimate) and computational complexity. Only two-stage least-squares will be discussed here.

Since two-stage least-squares was the method used to estimate the over-identified system describing the market for farmland, it is perhaps advisable to discuss the subject in terms of that model. The equations were

$$S = a + b_1 P + b_2 R + b_3 U + b_4 LF \qquad (8\text{–}22)$$

$$P = c + d_1 D + d_2 R + d_3 T + d_4 P/P_p + d_5 \\ UL + d_6 WPI \quad (8\text{–}23)$$

$$S = D \qquad (8\text{–}24)$$

The justification for the two-stage least-squares is the consideration that all of the variables in a simultaneous system influence in some way each of the endogenous variables. Thus, while S is directly related to R, U, and LF, since the system is simultaneous, it is also determined by T, P_r/P_p, UL, and WPI. The first stage takes this into account. In stage one, S is regressed on all the other exogenous variables in the system regardless of the equation in which the exogenous variables appear.

The equation estimated in stage one is of no particular interest to the forecaster. The computer uses it to prepare a new series of data, S. Stage two involves the direct estimation of the structural Equation (8–22), using $\hat{S}$ instead of S plus the original data for the other variables.

By a similar two-stage process Equation (8–23) is estimated. A series $\hat{P}$ is computed and the structural equation estimated directly. The reader should not decide from the above description that two-stage least-squares regression is a great deal of work. In most situations a computer is doing all the work, and only seconds of additional computing time are required. The results obtained in the farmland example are shown below:

$$S = - \quad 0.176P + \quad 0.264R - \quad 1.197UL + \quad 0.068LF \quad (8\text{–}32)$$
$$(+) \ (0.067) \ (+) \ (2.661) \ (-) \ (0.242) \quad (+) \ (0.032)$$

$$P = - \quad 3.512D + \quad 7.119R - \quad 1.161T + \quad 2.371P_r/P_p$$
$$(-) \ (0.77) \quad (-) \ (1.796) \ (+) \ (0.549) \ (+) \ (0.462)$$

$$+ \quad 4.34UL - \quad 3.187WPI \quad (8\text{–}33)$$
$$(+) \ (0.839) \ (+) \ (0.195)$$

Below each equation is some additional information. The numbers in parentheses are the standard errors of each coefficient. Instead of an exact t test, the rule of thumb that the coefficient should be twice the associated standard error may be used to check significance. The coefficient for LF in equation (8–32) and for T in Equation (8–33) are only borderline significant. The signs in the parentheses are expected on the basis of economic theory and general knowledge or the market for land. In Equation (8–32) it is expected that the sign of R should be $+$, as one would expect more land to be supplied to the market as the alternative earnings opportunity is better. At the same time, one would also expect the sign of P to be positive for the usual reasons for which one expects an upward-sloping supply curve. The opposite sign was obtained in this instance and in three others. Something must be wrong.

Multicolinearity. If the forecaster is sure that his model is correctly stated but he continues to get incorrect signs from his regression analysis, one thing he will check is the existence of multicolinearity (or intercorrelation). Multicolinearity means that two or more of the variables used are highly correlated. In effect, the same variable has been used twice. The results of this duplication are unpredictable—hence, the incorrect signs. A search of the table of simple correlation coefficients reveals this to be the case. The correlation between urban land (UL) and technology (T) is .98. This should not be surprising when one considers that both nonfarm uses of land and technology have advanced steadily during the period studied.

When multicolinearity exists, the forecaster is better off than the econometrician. The solution to multicolinearity is the deletion of one of the variables. This is troublesome to the econometrician, who wants to estimate the various coefficients. However, the forecaster wants an equation which will forecast the dependent variable, and, if one exogenous variable will do

TABLE 8-1

Simple Correlation Coefficients between Exogenous Variables

	R	U	LF	F	T	P_r/P_p	UL	WPI
R....................	1.0	.22	− .49	.35	− .59	− .26	− .58	− .21
U		1.0	− .20	.37	− .28	− .66	− .28	− .44
LF...................			1.0	− .42	.55	.10	.52	.36
F.....................				1.0	− .93	− .05	− .94	− .86
T.....................					1.0	.07	.98	.78
P_r/P_p..........						1.0	.01	.26
UL...................							1.0	.77
WPI..................								1.0

the work of two, so much the better. The choice of which variable to remove is arbitrary, and, if computer time is no object, the forecaster may try both ways.

In the study used as an example, the researchers were interested in the technology variable (T), so urban land (UL) was discarded. Before rerunning the regression, they replaced $LF =$ land in farms with $F =$ the number of farms. The results of the new model, also established by two-stages least-squares, are shown below.

$$S = 0.064\,P - 5.672\,R - 0.789\,U + .004\,F$$
$$ (.199) \quad (1.224) \quad\;\; (.188) \quad\;\; (.003) \qquad (8\text{--}34)$$

$$P = -1.943D + 8.315R + 1.699T + 0.757P_r/P_p$$
$$ (0.697) \quad (2.191) \quad (0.321) \quad (0.372)$$

$$+\ 0.379WPI \qquad\qquad (8\text{--}35)$$
$$(0.158)$$

The sign on the interest-rate variable continues to be "wrong" in both equations, but all others are now as expected. It is quite possible that the expected sign on R is incorrect and that the model should be respecified still further. The coefficients for P and F in Equation (8–34) and D in Equation (8–35) are not significantly different from zero in this formulation.

Larger Models

It is worth noting that many simultaneous forecasting models have far more than two equations. Most larger models are of the macroeconomy and as such are necessarily much larger.

The models are usually referred to by the names of their developers. One well known model is the Klein-Goldberger model, which survives in a number of metamorphoses.[4] A

---

[4] L. R. Klein and A. S. Goldberger, *An Econometric Model of the United States,* Amsterdam: North Holland Publishing Co., 1955. A good explanation of this model and instructions for use may be found in D. B. Suits, "Forecasting with an Econometric Model," *American Economic Review,* Vol. 52, March 1962, pp. 104–32.

newer model which has greater ability to forecast monetary and financial markets is the Federal Reserve—MIT model.[5] The above models range in size from thirty to fifty equations. One of the largest ever attempted was the Brookings model, which has over six hundred equations. Detailed discussion of such large models may be found in the references cited.

Some relatively smaller models are available. One quite small model was developed by Friend and Taubman.[6] The model consists of five structural equations and an identity. It is reproduced here as an example only. The coefficients would have to be updated for forecasting use.

$$\Delta C = .86 + .41(\Delta \tilde{Y}_p + \Delta Y_{Dt-1}) \qquad (8\text{--}36)$$

$$\Delta Y_D = \frac{1.7 + .57(\Delta \tilde{Y} - .10\Delta^2\tilde{Y})}{1 + t_p} - \frac{\Delta t_p}{1 + t_p} Y_{Dt-1} \qquad (8\text{--}37)$$

$$\Delta H = .35 + .06(\Delta \tilde{Y} - Y_{t-1}) + .58\Delta HS_{t-\frac{1}{2}} - .16\Delta PE^e \qquad (8\text{--}38)$$

$$\Delta PE = -.82 + .08(\Delta \tilde{Y} + \Delta Y_{t-1}) + .63\Delta PE^e \qquad (8\text{--}39)$$

$$\Delta I = 1.51 + .025\Delta S^e - 1.15 I_{t-1} + 1.7\Delta PE^e \qquad (8\text{--}40)$$

$$\Delta Y = \Delta C + \Delta H + \Delta PE + \Delta I + \Delta G' \qquad (8\text{--}41)$$

$C =$ consumption expenditures
$Y =$ gross national product
$H =$ residential construction expenditure
$HS =$ housing starts
$PE =$ plant and equipment expenditures
$I =$ nonfarm inventory investment
$S =$ business sales
$G' =$ government expenditures and net exports
$Y_D =$ disposable income
$t_p =$ average personal tax rate

[5] F. deLeeuw, and E. M. Gramlich, "The Federal Reserve-MIT Econometric Model," *Federal Reserve Bulletin,* Jan. 1968, pp. 11–40, and R. H. Rasche and H. T. Shapiro, "The F.R.B.—M.I.T. Econometric Model: Its Special Features," *American Economic Review,* Vol. 58, May 1968, pp. 123–48.

[6] I. Friend, and P. Taubman, "A Short-Term Forecasting Model," *Review of Economics and Statistics,* Vol. 44, August 1964, pp. 229–36.

The $\triangle$ means that the change in the level of the variable is to be forecast. First differences were used in the estimation process. The $t-1$ refers to lagged values of the variable named. A $\sim$ over a variable means that the actual data on a variable have been replaced by the forecast value from the first stage of the two-stage least-squares regression procedure. A superscript e after a variable indicates the expected values of the variable. The expected values must be estimated by other techniques.

The forecast is prepared in the usual manner. The lagged values are known. The forecaster prepares estimates of $\triangle PE^{e}$, $\triangle S^{e}$, and $\triangle G$ and solves the system to obtain forecasts of $\triangle Y_{D}$, $\triangle H$, $\triangle PE$, $\triangle I$, and $\triangle Y$. Of course, the coefficients should be updated as new data become available. The coefficients shown were only valid at a time in the past.

PROBLEM

1. Solve problem one from Chapter 7 again, using a parabola this time. Plot both the linear and the nonlinear equations on graph paper and compare the two. From a visual inspection decide which most closely fits the observed data points.

REFERENCES

The reader should also consult the references to Chapter 7 for sources of information on topics treated in this chapter.

BASS, F. M. "A Simultaneous Equation Regression Study of Advertising and Sales of Cigarettes." *Journal of Marketing Research,* Vol. VI, No. 3 (August, 1969), pp. 291–300.

CZAMANSKI, S. A. "A Method of Forecasting Metropolitan Growth by Means of Distributed Lags Analysis. *Journal of Regional Science,* Vol. VI, No. 1 (Summer, 1965).

RASCHE, ROBERT H., and SHAPIRO, HAROLD T. "The F.R.B.-M.I.T.

Econometric Model: Its Special Features." *American Economic Review,* Vol. LVIII, No. 2 (May, 1968), pp. 123–49.

SUITS, DANIEL B. "Forecasting With an Econometric Model." *American Economic Review,* Vol. LII, No. 1 (March, 1962), pp. 104–32.

TOMEK, WILLIAM G. "Using Zero-One Variables with Time-Series Data in Regression Equations" *Journal of Farm Economics,* Vol. XLV, No. 4 (November, 1963), pp. 814–22.

chapter
—9—
Forecasting: Art and Science

The statement was made in Chapter 1 that forecasting is still an art form. The intervening chapters may have left the impression that art has taken a back seat. Yet, despite the large amounts of mathematics displayed in the interior of this text, it is necessary to consider once again the art of the forecaster.

Three aspects of the art of forecasting are considered in the chapter below. First, the role of the forecaster in his organization is developed in sufficiently general terms as to be applicable to many types of organizations. The second portion of the chapter treats the factors which a forecaster must consider in his choice among competing forecasting models. Finally, the troublesome question of how good a record a particular forecasting model has made is discussed in terms of formal techniques for evaluating forecasts.

The Role of the Forecaster[1]

The discussion below will be directly related to the role of the forecaster in business situations. However, it would not be too difficult to substitute "legislature," "Senate Committee," or "school board" for "management" or "board of directors" in every instance. The results would be little changed.

Ultimately the role of the forecaster comes down to communication to the appropriate administrators information which they would not otherwise have and which will lead to improved decisions. This statement has many dimensions which must be examined in turn.

Communication alone is difficult. The forecaster must use terms that management will understand. The technical jargon of forecasting will not serve well when directed to someone interested only in profit next quarter. Dumping a large amount of computer output on the boardroom table will impress the board members but not be of much help in their decision making. The management must be able to understand.

The other side of this coin, however, is the need for the communication to be precisely related to the decision at hand. Is the requirement for general business conditions in the future? The forecast should be in terms of gross national product, unemployment rates, interest rates, and/or prices. Such forecasts may be for the economy as a whole but should also be interpreted in terms of the community or region in which the firm operates.

But, if the forecast is to be specific, it must be just that. It should be in terms of the correct units—dollar sales or physical units. The forecast should be for a specific product, as listed

---

[1] For more detailed treatment of the points made below, see the excellent papers by W. H. Chartener, W. E. Hoadley, and R. P. Ulin in W. F. Butler and R. A. Kavesh, eds., *How Business Economists Forecast*, Englewood Cliffs, N.J.: Prentice Hall, 1966.

in a catalog, rather than for an industry-wide group of products. And, if products are sold in separate markets, then a market-by-market breakdown may be required.

Forecasts at the Functional Level. Not all forecasts are intended for use by top management. In large conglomerate corporations forecasts must be prepared for the diverse parts of the firm. Frequently the divisions of a conglomerate are virtually independent in operation, and forecasts for the parent firm must be contingent upon forecasts for the divisions.

Even the various agencies of the federal government require forecasts tailored to the decision level. For example, the cabinet agencies which operate field offices need separate information for each of the ten regions in which the offices are located. An agency such as the Appalachian Regional Development Commission requires forecasts related to the region served. Considerable interest currently attaches to the development of state and regional input-output tables which may be useful for a variety of purposes.

Regardless of the size of the unit, some forecasts must be specifically tailored to the requirements of particular functions or functional units. The forecaster must be alert to these requirements. Of course, in smaller firms or agencies forecasters operating as such may not exist, and the personnel of the functional unit may have to prepare the forecasts.

The preparation of sales forecasts by the marketing department has already been discussed. In some instances, when the firm has employed a logistics system, the marketing forecasts become inputs to decisions as to which warehouse location and which transportation system to employ. Many production departments now employ sophisticated decision technology requiring accurate forecasts. The production department therefore needs or must prepare forecasts on prices of inputs and outputs, quantities required, and inventory levels. Also, it has been shown that by coordinating their decisions, perhaps based on common forecasts, the marketing and production departments may achieve higher order optimization.[2]

The finance department must have or prepare forecasts of a wide variety of interest rates in order to decide which financial strategy to employ. Forecasts of cash flows are required for the preparation of the proforma balance sheet. Any capital budgeting analysis requires forecasts of the revenue stream generated by the investment project and perhaps a forecast of the discount rate as well.

Information-systems analysts are primarily engaged in providing data inputs into the other departments. However, in planning the information system to employ—particularly the hardware components—they require forecasts of the growth or decline of the firm. Manpower forecasts are of much interest and are increasingly used by industrial-relations specialists. Forecasts of technology change are similarly employed.

Other Considerations. It should not even be necessary to point out that the forecasts mentioned above must be prepared by the time the decision is to be made. On occasion, the forecaster may even have to anticipate what information will be required.

The forecasts should be in terms which are appropriate to the decision technique employed. If the forecast is to be used by an operations research group, it must be precise, or the variance should be stated. As mentioned before, if the forecast is for top management, it should concern the variables in which they are interested.

It is important to consider the variance of the forecast. Some techniques provide the forecaster with an estimate of the variance, while in other cases the forecaster must construct *a priori* variance estimates. He must then translate the variance

---

[2] M. F. Tuite, "Merging Marketing Strategy Selection and Production Scheduling: A Higher Order Optimum," *Journal of Industrial Engineering,* February 1968, pp. 76–84.

into management terms. In particular, what is the worst outcome that is likely to happen? Or, since success requires contingency planning as well, how much better might we do? An informal sensitivity analysis of this type could be very useful to top management.

Two-Way Street. If management expects to receive effective communication, it must in turn communicate. The forecaster must have access to the thinking if not the deliberations of management. In this way he may know precisely what problems are of concern, and he is alerted to those strategies of management which are designed to assure that some forecasts become incorrect.

The most effective direct communication from management to the forecaster would be a precise statement of required forecasts and how these fit into the activities of the firm. However, this is still less satisfactory than direct and constant contact.

Management should also communicate the precise part that the forecaster is expected to play in the firm's profit potential. The forecaster may then be held accountable for his contribution net of costs and rewarded and/or punished accordingly. Finally, the forecasting unit should not be a dead-end position. The forecaster will be more effective if he knows that his actions will lead to promotion to higher levels of management.

External Communications. Since communications of information are the forecaster's only product, sources of information are especially important to him. Communication more or less horizontally is therefore to be fostered. Management may aid in this endeavor by making it possible for the forecaster to be out of the office as required.

Development of data sources is a must for the forecaster. The most essential group of data sources is the myriad of published data sources. But the expert forecaster can, by private communications with others, extract data which is not published.

The forecaster must also be in constant communication with his professional colleagues. Though this means he may continually improve his practice of the art and science of forecasting. Further, by compiling other forecasts, he may check his own results. In fact, the compilation itself may be valuable, especially if the forecasts are of macroeconomic variables.

Revisions. The communication process does not end with the forecast. Forecasting is an ongoing process. An important role of the forecaster is to prevent surprises to management which are the result of changes in the condition of the firm or the economy. On the other hand, it may be just as important to assure management that present conditions will continue.

The most obvious time for a revision is when it seems that the forecast is in error. Some forecasting systems have built-in warning signals that flag any variable which strays more than some predetermined tolerance from the forecast value. In other instances, the forecaster must perform such a function by personal surveillance. Either way, the existence of the error must be communicated along with the reason for it. Obviously, management response will be different for an unforeseen change in the economy than for erroneous construction of the forecasting model.

Detection of error is not the only reason forecasts should be revised. Many forecasts have built-in plans for revision based either on appearance of new data or on the passage of some specified time period. The time period need not be constant. Long-term forecasts are revised at decreasing intervals as the period of the forecast approaches.

Alternative Models and Approaches

Another part of the art of the forecaster lies in his choice of applications of the science. This text has indicated some of the diversity of forecasting models. How does the forecaster choose which to use? Personal preference? Cost? Elegance? Ease of use? Accuracy? The economist would say to use the one which contributes to profit because the marginal reward exceeds the marginal cost. There is something to be said for that position, but doesn't accuracy count for something?

It turns out that suitability of the model for the job to be done has several dimensions, one of which is cost versus results. Some of the other dimensions will be discussed in this section. The measurement of accuracy is a separable topic and will be left for the next section.

The question of cost has been dealt with in the introduction. For some purposes, the simplest models suffice, apart from the question of accuracy. In other situations highly complex and sophisticated models are in order. But the cost of a model is not easily ascertained, and there is room for disagreement. Even in a situation where the forecaster allows himself the luxury of a complex model, he must still choose among several. The following discussion is not designed to lead the forecaster to a particular choice but will serve to illuminate some of the choice criteria.

Opportunistic-Econometric. Despite outward appearance, it is difficult to dichotomize the discussion of these approaches without vastly overstating the position of those who would defend one model or the other. A little overstatement will be indulged in here in order to sharpen the discussion.

If one adopts the concept of the economist, which is to measure the cost in terms of opportunity cost (i.e., what is given up), then the cost of an econometric model may be a loss of flexibility.[3] An opportunistic model is not a matter of simply borrowing liberally from most other techniques and using any kind of existing outlook information. The tech-

[3] J. P. Lewis and R. C. Turner, *Business Conditions Analysis,* 2d ed., New York: McGraw-Hill, 1967, pp. 388–90.

nique, as described in an earlier chapter, follows the national income accounting framework and thus qualifies as a true model. But, at the same time, it is possible to incorporate even judgment and pure hunches.

The shortcomings of the econometric approach are two. First, in order to capture all the interactions, the econometric model must have many equations. As more equations are added, the model becomes more cumbersome to use in terms of both the initial estimation and later the maintenance. The second and more telling difficulty is the structural rigidity of the econometric model. The forecast becomes model-bound; then structural changes in the economy can no longer be introduced.

Of course, those who favor the econometric approach and view the term "opportunistic" in its pejorative sense would say that the cost of the opportunistic model is that it is inexplicit and overly simple and lacks a framework for using a variety of empirical analysis.[4] The complexity of an econometric model would be a burden if it were not that the economy is itself complex and only a model of equal complexity can resolve the conflicting elements and arrive at a reasonable forecast.

The explicitness of an econometric forecast leads to a number of desirable characteristics. The first is transferability. It can be written down and passed along to others. Second, it is free from hunches and guesses, in that the entire structure and all assumptions are in full view. If there is disagreement, the portion of the model over which there is disagreement may be changed. The new forecast is then but a matter of seconds away via the electronic computer.

---

[4] Anderson, W. H. L., "The Michigan Econometric Forecast: The Outlook for Gross National Product in 1963," *Economic Outlook,* pp. 34–50.

Since the econometric model is a series of simultaneous equations, each may be studied in turn. All the economics literature and underlying research may be used in specifying each equation in turn. When new research results become available, they may be readily incorporated into the existing framework.

Finally, Suits points out that, since there is a system of equations, there is an equation for each unknown.[5] As every high school algebra student knows, it is possible to substitute an identity for that equation. Thus, if it is thought that the historical relationships used to estimate the equation for plant and equipment expenditures result in a less reliable forecast than those of the McGraw-Hill investment plans survey, the forecaster need only remove the equation and substitute the survey result. The forecaster may also employ judgment to change the parameters of an equation to reflect a change in say, the tax laws. Thus, there is no lack of flexibility in the econometric approach.

Of course, Lewis and Turner would—and do—say that this then is no longer an econometric model but an opportunistic one.[6] The tampering with coefficients or use of survey data transforms the econometric model in an opportunistic model at least in part. By saying this, they bring nearly every forecaster in existence into the camp of the "good guys" as they define it.

Quarter-Annually. The arguments presented by Suits above referred to an econometric model based on annual data, though he would in all probability defend other econometric models similarly. Yet Nerlove points out that another dimension of cost may arise when annual models are employed.[7] It is argued

---

[5] Suits, *op. cit.*, p. 106–7.

[6] Lewis and Turner, *op. cit.*, p. 390.

[7] M. Nerlove, "A Quarterly Econometric Model for the United Kingdom," *American Economic Review*, Vol. 52, March 1962, pp. 154–76.

in Nerlove's article that on several counts quarterly models may be superior—i.e., lower cost.

First, there is the question of validity of the assumptions of the model versus the number of data points required for estimation of a large econometric model. For a model of any complexity at all, the forecaster requires large numbers of observations in order to estimate the equations using regression techniques. For annual models it becomes necessary to use data over many years. But, if the forecaster is forced to use data from, say, 1900 to the present in order to get enough observations, the assumption that there have been no structural changes in the economy is almost certainly violated. For a quarterly model it is at least possible to start in the post–World War II era and still obtain enough observations for estimation purposes. However, because of seasonality and other difficulties, it is not quite true that quarterly data result in four times as many observations as annual data over a given time span.

Second, annual models may not allow the forecaster to analyze adequately the subtle changes in an economy which are time related. In recent U.S. history, business fluctuations have been so short-lived that annual observations could miss much of the change in activity. Policy has become so sensitive that a particular monetary or fiscal policy action could be reversed within a year. Only a quarterly model will allow the forecaster to deal with policy measures which may not have an impact for six to nine months after they are initiated. Thus, it is seen that another cost of relying on an annual model may be its insensitivity to short-run changes in the economy.

Another cost Nerlove attributes to the use of annual model is its inability to provide what may best be called intermediate-term forecasts needed by policy makers and businessmen. For the very short range, simpler forecasts may suffice and an econometric model is inappropriate. For the longer term investment decisions, an annual model will do very well if it has been correctly estimated. But many business and policy decisions relate to a three- to ten-month time horizon. For these a quarterly model is clearly superior.

Large-Small. Models, be they opportunistic or econometric, annual or quarterly, may quickly grow to gargantuan size as the forecaster seeks to improve his model. Everyone knows that it is more work to handle the larger model. Taubman argues the costs may be more than the labor input and that the forecaster should prefer the smallest possible model which will give all the information desired.[8]

The choice criteria may be stated as follows: (1) The model must forecast all of the relevant variables. (2) The forecast must be available within specified time periods, which may be quite short. (3) The forecasts must be of high quality. The first may be inconsistent with the second and third. In many instances the additional information may actually be a nuisance, then meeting the second and third criteria becomes paramount.

It is important to point out that the time-consuming features of larger models are no longer their estimation and solution. Once the parameters are estimated and the exogenous variables are determined, a twenty-five to thirty-equation Klein-Goldberger model can be solved in 12 milliseconds. The over-600-equation Brookings model can be solved for eight quarters into the future in 2½ minutes on a well known third-generation, hybrid computer.

Two other phases of forecasting with larger models do require significant amounts of time. First, data collection and processing is a large effort. Even if a forecaster has an adequate staff who are close to data sources and spend all their

---

[8] P. Taubman, "Small vs. Large Models as Forecasting Tools," Talk before the Chicago Chapter, American Statistical Association Annual Forecasting Conference, University of Illinois at Chicago Circle, June 15, 1967.

time on data collection, preparation of data for a large model could require a week's effort. Second, there is the problem of adjusting constants. Even if the model has been used in the past and has been estimated with the most recent data, when it becomes time to actually prepare a forecast, a forecaster will want to consider the coefficients carefully. Perhaps an equation has not performed well in past forecasts, a law has been passed which changes conditions, or anticipations surveys indicate that the past data are not valid for future predictions. The constants must then be adjusted to compensate, but this takes time. Further, because of the simultaneous nature of the model, the difficulty of making such adjustments increases faster than the number of equations in the model.

It is also possible that smaller models may actually provide forecasts of better quality. One reason models grow large is that the forecaster has sought disaggregation in an attempt to gain information. Disaggregation may be very useful where important nonlinearities and multicolinearity exist, but other problems are introduced.

Many of the disaggregated data series are not available as such. As a result, the total or aggregated series must be allocated by ratios and interpolated to intercensus years. This process may greatly add to errors of measurement and the variance of the error. Further, the errors may well be compounded where existing stocks are estimated by accumulating past (erroneous) data series.

Another way that models grow is by the addition of explanatory variables to various equations. Since these variables may be difficult to handle as exogenous variables, equations are added which make the variables endogenous, but this procedure does not solve anything. For identification purposes the additional equations must also contain exogenous variables, yet these may be even more difficult to forecast. Thus the forecaster has (maybe) gained in quantity of information at a loss in quality.

Finally, if the above reasons have not been convincing as to the loss of quality in large models, there is one more statement of difficulty. A formal proof is required to demonstrate precisely the nature of the final difficulty. However, the policy of sparing the reader formal proofs will be continued and only the results stated.

The essence of the argument is this. In large models, most forecasters and econometricians begin working on each equation in turn, trying to achieve a high R^2. If n represents the number of different equations tested (and in a good study n will be large), the forecaster has a substantial job obtaining the best specification of any one equation.

But, because of the simultaneous nature of the model, the testing should not be in isolation. The forecaster will probably want to test more than one version of the model. If there are m variants of the model and n variants of each equation, then there are m^n tests which the forecaster must attempt. Since n should be large, the number of equations should be small so that m remains small; otherwise the number of tests to be performed will be impossible.

Another way of saying this is to admit that, because of nonlinearities and multicolinearities, there exists a large, disaggregated model which will be of higher quality and contain more information than a smaller model; but, because of the amount of search involved, it is probable that a best small model may be found, while it is unlikely that the best large model may be found. Thus, the forecaster using the small model may wind up with higher quality than the forecaster with the large model, because the latter has failed to find his best specification of the large model.

Lest the above discussion be taken as a one-sided argument

for smaller models, it is important to note that the individual forecaster still retains a choice. If the time and quality variables are unimportant to the particular forecaster, he should opt for the additional information of a larger model. However, he should bear in mind the costs involved.

Formal Evaluation Techniques

The above discussion may well have left the potential forecaster uneasy. Even after presented with the choice criteria, he may want to examine some objective evaluations of alternative forecasting techniques. The following paragraphs will attempt to provide the guidelines he needs.

Three evaluation techniques are presented here. The first is in the form of a check list. A forecaster could use it to evaluate either a new model he was in the process of developing or an existing model, either his own or someone else's. The second method is a statistical technique for evaluating a model against itself or against other models. Finally, the National Bureau of Economic Research has undertaken a project of evaluating alternative forecast techniques through a survey of forecasters. The results of their work will be discussed.

Check List.   Chartener suggests the following points as items of interest to the forecaster attempting to evaluate a forecast.[9] The two main items to be checked are the data and the model with its attendant assumptions.

The questions to be asked about the data are as follows: (1) Is the source reliable and accurate? (2) Since more than one source may qualify under question 1, is the source used the best? (3) Are the data the most recent available? (4) If yes to question 3, are the data subject to subsequent revision? and (5) Is there any known systematic bias in the data which may be dealt with? Of course, many data sources will meet

---

[9] Chartener, in Butler and Kavesh, *op. cit.,* p. 524.

only some of the criteria. The forecaster must be aware of the shortcomings of his data sources and act accordingly.

The model and assumptions should be similarly examined. The model should be examined for its internal logic and reasonableness. If possible, it should be grounded in economic and/or behavioral theory. But the model may work only by accident. If so, this should be made clear, and some determination of whether the relationship will hold in the future is required.

The assumptions should be clearly stated, implied, or obvious; reasonable; internally consistent; and complete. It is also necessary to consider the possibility that there might be another set of assumptions which would meet the above criteria but which would yield a different forecast.

Not every forecast technique is going to meet all of the above. This does not mean that a technique is useless. Nor does the fact that a forecast meets the criteria guarantee that it will perform well. The performance of a forecast which has been previously used can be checked against its own record or against that of other forecasts. Such tests are discussed below.

The U Statistic. There is a number of statistical forecast evaluators of which Theil's U statistic is only one. Devising such a scoring device is in some ways easier than deciding on the standard of comparison. Two standards may be identified.

First, one could compare the forecast being evaluated with a naïve forecast to see if there are vast differences. The comparison would be against a naïve forecast such as same as last year, same change as last year, or some average trend. The naïve forecast could be the output of an exponential smoothing model or the result of fitting some simple cycle model to past data. Presumably, one could even gather a collection of forecasts and use the consensus as a standard of comparison.

In the second case, the forecast may be compared against

the outcome when there is enough history to do so. The comparison may be against the actual level of the variable forecast, or the change observed may be compared with the change forecast. Other evaluation techniques consider the number of turning points correctly forecast. Finally, the ability to forecast acceleration or deceleration may be examined.

The Theil U statistic is based on a comparison of the predicted change with the observed change.[10] It is defined as

$$U = \frac{\sqrt{\frac{1}{n}\sum_{i}^{n}(P_i - A_i)^2}}{\sqrt{\frac{1}{n}\sum_{i}^{n}P_i^2} + \sqrt{\frac{1}{n}\sum_{i}^{n}A_i^2}} \qquad (9\text{--}1)$$

where the P_i are the forecasts for each period, the A_i are the observed values for the same period, and n is the number of periods being compared.

The denominator of this statistic normalizes it so that its domain is the closed interval of zero to one.[11] Obviously, $U = 0$ is a perfect forecast, since the forecast would equal actual and $P_i - A_i = 0$ for all i. At the other extreme, $U = 1$ would be a case of all incorrect forecasts. Figure 9–1 below helps explain erroneous forecasts.

This diagram is the same as the one in Chapter 1. The line of perfect forecasts results in $U = 0$. Zones IB and IIIB are zones of under-prediction of actual changes. Similarly, zones IA and IIIA are zones of over-prediction of actual change. If most of the points fall in these regions, $0 < U < 1$ will obtain. Zones II and IV are zones of turning-point errors —i.e., predicted increase when in fact there was a decrease and

---

[10] H. Theil, *Economic Forecasts and Policy*, Amsterdam: North Holland Publishing Co., 1965, pp. 32–38.

[11] Unless $P_i = 0$, $A_i = 0$ Vi in which case U is undefined.

vice versa. Even if all the points were in these zones, U would not equal one, though it would be getting close.

In order to have a score of one, the points would have to lie not only in Zones II and IV but on a line such as the one labeled $U = 1$ in Figure 9–1. The only other place where points could be found and still have $U = 1$ would be along the horizontal and vertical axis.

FIGURE 9–1

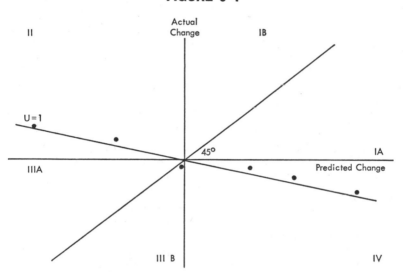

The U statistic is sensitive to additive transformations of any series of P_i and A_i. That is, take any series of P_i and A_i and add a large constant, say 1000, to each. Now compute U and the correlation coefficient for each. The correlation coefficient will be the same for each. The U statistic will be larger for the series than it will be for the series plus 1000. This is as it should be. It is easy to forecast small changes. Thus, as in golf, it is necessary to be more accurate in order to obtain a low score.[12]

[12] Ridker, R. G., "An Evaluation of the Forecasting Ability of the Norwegian National Budgeting System," *Review of Economics and Statistics*, Vol. 45, February 1963, p. 27.

The numerator is the key to the U statistic. It can be decomposed for further analysis of the nature of any forecast errors which might exist. The decomposition is

$$\frac{1}{n} \sum_{i}^{n} (P_i - A_i)^2 = (\bar{P} - \bar{A})^2 + (S_p - S_a)^2$$

$$+ 2(1 - r)S_p S_a \quad (9\text{--}2)$$

where $\bar{P}$ and $\bar{A}$ are the means of each of the series, S_p and S_a are standard deviations of each series, and r is the correlation coefficient between the series.

Each of the several portions may contribute to U being greater than zero. The first part, $(\bar{P} - \bar{A})^2$, will be zero if the observed pairs of P_i and A_i are centered around the line of perfect forecasts. The failure to do so is termed systematic errors by forecasters. Systematic error implies that $(\bar{P} - \bar{A})^2 > 0$, while the desired condition is $(\bar{P} - \bar{A})^2 = 0$. Attempts to correct for this type of systematic error by a simple transformation of the results may succeed but perhaps at the cost of worsened results on other scores.[13]

Another error would arise if $(S_p - S_a)^2$ did not equal zero, the desired value. This term will equal zero if a regression line through the pairs of P_i and A_i is at least parallel to the line of perfect forecasts if not coincident with it.

On the other hand, $2(1 - r)S_p S_a$ is a measure of covariation, and the desired value of this term is 1. When the value of this term gets close to one, the forecast and actual changes are shown to be in the same direction and of similar magnitude. If plotted on a chart such as Figure 9–1, the points would lie along a line which would be parallel to, though not necessarily on top of, the line of perfect forecasts. This would mean

---

[13] Sims, C. A., "Evaluating Short-Term, Macro-Economic Forecasts: The Durch Performance," *Review of Economics and Statistics*, Vol. 49, May 1967, p. 839.

that the model is in general working well and that one need only make those corrections which will shift the observed pattern of forecasts to coincide with the line of perfect forecasts. At the other extreme, if this term $[2(1-r)S_pS_a]$ is near zero, there is no relationship between the forecast and the actual value of the variables, and the forecaster is simply making mistakes.

The evaluation process via the U statistics may better be understood through an example. Consider the following equation, used to forecast the interest rate on Aaa seasoned corporate bonds (R_c).

$$R_c = 1.1225 + .337R_{cp} + \sum_i^{18} w_i R_{cp-i} \qquad (9\text{--}3)$$

$w_1 = .024$	$w_7 = .064$	$w_{13} = .023$
$w_2 = .015$	$w_8 = .059$	$w_{14} = .018$
$w_3 = .041$	$w_9 = .052$	$w_{15} = .012$
$w_4 = .057$	$w_{10} = .044$	$w_{16} = .012$
$w_5 = .065$	$w_{11} = .036$	$w_{17} = .009$
$w_6 = .067$	$w_{12} = .029$	$w_{18} = .005$

This equation is only one of the many in the MIT–Federal Reserve model mentioned above. Since Equation (9–3) forecasts one endogenous variable (R_C) as a function of two exogenous variables, the interest rate on commercial paper (R_{cp}), in two forms Equation (9–3) may be taken out and evaluated separately here, though the significance of the test is lessened.

Figure 9–2 shows the values forecast by this model in comparison with those observed. Clearly the two series moved together. In the latter part of 1968, the forecast and actual values moved in opposite directions in two successive quarters. Further, in the fourth quarter of 1967, the absolute error in level was 2.7 interest points. Is this a good or bad forecast? It would be difficult to evaluate such a result without a technique such as the U statistic.

Plotting the forecast change versus the predicted change

FIGURE 9–2
Prediction Results

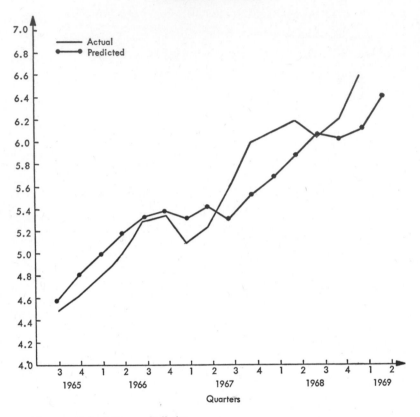

Source: *Federal Reserve Bulletins.*

gives the result shown in Figure 9–3. Most of the points are in the first quadrant, equally divided between under- and over-prediction. Only three represent turning-point errors.

The computed U value for the forecasts is $U = .025$. This value is much closer to zero than one but difficult to evaluate in isolation. As a simple comparison, a least-squares trend line may fit through the observed data points. For this line the value of the statistic is $U = .014$. Thus, the forecast does not do as well as the naïve forecast.

Table 9–1 shows the decomposed portions of the numerator

of the U statistic for Equation 9–3. Note that with a U of .025 most of the values do indeed approach the desired values. But an interesting comparison arises. The naïve model has a $(\bar{P} - \bar{A})^2$ of 0.0008, which means that there is a greater systematic error about the mean for the simple trend equation. Equa-

TABLE 9–1

Component	Desired	Computed
$(\bar{P} - \bar{A})^2$............	0	.0007
$(S_p - S_a)^2$............	0	.0002
$2(1 - r)\, S_a S_p$.........	1	.999

tion (9–3) apparently contains less systematic error of this type but fails on other grounds.

Comparisons of Many Forecasts

The National Bureau of Economic Research has shown interest in evaluating forecasts prepared in business environments. A benchmark study has been published. This study analyzed existing forecasts back to the early 1950's. A continuing service of collecting and evaluating forecasts has been instituted.

The results of the study must be considered tentative, to be confirmed by the ongoing work.[14] However, some of the preliminary findings are quite interesting.

Eighty-four forecasts were analyzed. The results are shown below in Table 9–2. The GNP figure is the first published estimate which is thought to correspond most closely to the data the forecasters used as inputs in their forecasts. Subsequent

[14] Zarnowitz, V., *An Appraisal of Short-Term Economic Forecasts,* New York: National Bureau of Economic Research, Occasional Paper 104, 1967.

TABLE 9-2

GNP, Error of First Estimate of GNP, and Errors of Forecasts and Extrapolations, with and without Sign, 1953–63. (billion dollars)

	1953	1954	1955	1956	1957	1958	1959	1960	1961	1962	1963	Average Error All Years Signed	Average Error All Years Absolute
First estimate, GNP	367.2	357.2	387.2	412.4	434.4	437.7	479.5	503.2	521.3	553.9	585.0		
Error of first estimate	+ 2.6	− 7.6	−10.8	− 6.8	− 6.7	− 9.6	− 4.1	+ 0.6	+ 1.2	− 6.4	4.2	− 4.7	5.5
Forecast error, signed	−11.1	− 1.4	−19.5	−10.8	− 6.3	+ 2.6	−10.7	+ 7.4	− 9.8	+ 8.7	−12.9	− 5.2	
Forecast error, absolute	11.1	6.7	19.5	10.8	6.6	4.3	11.5	7.4	10.2	8.7	15.0		10.0
Error, extrapolation of level of last year ($Y_{t+1} = Y_t$)	−19.2	+ 7.7	−26.7	−21.5	−19.7	+ 2.6	−37.8	−21.1	−16.9	−35.2	−30.3	−19.8	21.7
Error, extrapolation of trend	− 3.6	+34.2	−14.7	− 3.5	− 3.8	+19.3	−23.0	− 4.3	− 0.1	−10.1	−11.4	− 1.9	11.6

revisions changed the figure by one half to over ten billion dollars, as shown in the second row.

The third and fourth rows of the table contain the average forecast errors. In row three, minus signs predominate. On balance the forecasts were low. As may be seen in row two, most of the first estimates of GNP were also low, so the final estimates of GNP were somewhat higher. Comparison of the forecasts with GNP as ultimately determined would result in the errors being even larger on the low side. The absolute size of the errors ranged from slightly over four billion to almost twenty billion. The average of the ten years was ten billion. GNP in this period ranged from 358 to 585. The error was less than 2 percent of its average level.

The naïve forecasts did not do well at all. Errors of more than 30 billion are recorded. Yet, the average absolute error (11.6 billion), for an extrapolation of the average trend was only slightly higher than that of the forecasts tested.

However, the change in GNP was predicted with considerably less accuracy. The error was approximately 40 percent of the variable forecast. A scatter diagram is shown in Figure 9–3.

The change in GNP recorded, both initially and as revised, are shown in Table 9–3. The average change forecast by the 84 forecasters is shown in the next row. The ten-year average predicted changes, 17.3 signed and 19.2 absolute, were both underestimates of the actual change. The errors in the forecast compared with the first estimate of actual are contained in the next row. The average absolute error was just over 8 billion.

The extrapolation of the average trend did no better in predicting changes in GNP and produced two turning-point errors compared with only one for the forecasters. The error for the extrapolation averaged 9.3 billion over the ten years, about 45 percent of the variable forecast, even though the average forecast was closer to the actual average change. The

FIGURE 9–3

Actual and Predicted Changes

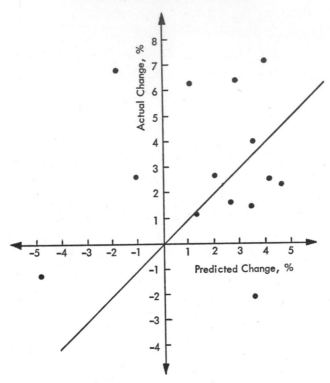

Source: *Federal Reserve Bulletins,* computer outputs.

errors, while balancing out, were very large when they oc-curred.

The use of average errors tends to hide some of the uncer-tainty associated with the forecasts. There is some dispersion around the average. During the decade studied the dispersion was from 7 to 14 billion dollars on the GNP estimate. Never-theless, the forecast of GNP was better than the naïve forecasts and better than the forecasts of components of GNP. However, there was some indication that when experts in a particular area—say, government expenditures—prepared a forecast of that variable, these forecasts could be combined to produce a

TABLE 9-3

Changes in GNP, Changes in GNP Forecast and Extrapolated and Errors in Prediction, 1953–1963. (billion dollars)

	Actual and Predicted Changes and Errors											Average Predicted Changes and Errors	
	1952 –53	1953 –54	1954 –55	1955 –56	1956 –57	1957 –58	1958 –59	1959 –60	1960 –61	1961 –62	1962 –63	Signed	Absolute
Change in GNP													
First estimate......	19.2	– 7.7	26.7	21.5	19.7	– 2.6	37.8	21.1	16.9	35.2	30.3	19.8	21.7
Revised............	19.1	.2	33.2	21.2	21.9	6.2	36.3	20.2	16.3	40.2	28.9	22.2	22.2
Predicted change, Average 44 forecasts............	10.6	–12.5	11.0	14.5	16.8	4.6	32.2	30.5	7.4	43.3	18.6	17.3	19.2
Average error of forecasts...........	– 8.6	– 4.8	–15.7	– 7.0	– 2.9	+ 7.2	– 5.6	+ 9.4	– 9.5	+ 8.1	–11.7	– 3.1	8.2
Extrapolated change...	19.6	20.7	15.5	21.7	19.9	20.4	21.6	18.4	16.8	25.3	20.5	20.0	20.0
Error of extrapolation..	+ 0.4	+28.4	–11.2	+ 0.2	+ 0.2	+23.0	–16.2	– 2.7	– 0.1	– 9.9	– 9.8	+ 0.2	9.3

superior GNP forecast even though the interdependencies were neglected.

Quarterly GNP forecasts were superior to extrapolations up to three quarters out, but from four quarters on there was no longer demonstrable superiority. There was no indication that the errors increased systematically as the time period was extended. In fact, the error was as likely to decrease as to increase. Multiperiod forecasts typically had dismal records of forecasting turning points.

Personal consumption expenditures were more correctly forecast than government expenditures, which in turn were better than gross private domestic investment. It was felt that the greatest need for improvement was in residential construction, inventory change, and net foreign investment. Use of plant and equipment survey results was found to improve the forecasts of capital expenditures. The greatest scope for improvement was in consumption, including nondurables and services. The forecasts were far worse than the simple extrapolations.

Where does all this leave the forecaster? The forecasts were clearly superior to naïve projections, yet there is obviously room for improvement. One of the recommendations of the study was that forecasters could improve their forecasts by simply keeping a record of their forecasts, the estimated present position, and the techniques employed and analyzing these records.[15]

To this end, the Business and Economic Statistics Section of the American Statistical Association and the NBER have begun a survey of forecasters.[16] The intent is to provide an objective and systematic record which will provide the information needed for evaluation and improvement of forecasting techniques. NBER will tabulate the forecasts as reported on a

---

[15] *Ibid.,* p. 8.

[16] V. Zarnowitz, "The New ASA-NBER Survey of Forecast, by Economic Statisticians," *The American Statistician,* Vol. 23, Feb. 1969.

questionnaire, compute measures of error and other relevant statistics, and perform such analysis as seems reasonable. In particular, there will be a track record against which to compare new forecast techniques, to study probabilistic forecasts, and to analyze the degree of consensus among forecasters. Thus, a valuable service will be performed, and it may be expected that future forecasts will be improved.

REFERENCES

ÅBERG, C. J. "Forecasts, Uncertainty and Decision Making." *Swedish Journal of Economics,* Vol. LXIV, December, 1967.

CARLSON, J. A. "Forecasting Errors and Business Cycles." *American Economic Review,* Vol. LVII, June, 1967, pp. 363–78.

CLARK, JOHN J. *The Management of Forecasting.* New York: St. John's University Press, 1969.

COLE, R. *Errors in Provisional Estimates of Gross National Product.* New York: National Bureau of Economic Research, 1970.

DEDERICK, R. G. "Problems of a Practitioner in Business Forecasting." *Business Economics,* Vol. I, Winter, 1965–66.

HAASE, P. E. "Technological Change and Manpower Forecasts." *Industrial Relations,* Vol. V, May, 1966.

KEMP, M. C. "Economic Forecasting when the Subject of the Forecast Is Influenced by the Forecast." *American Economic Review,* Vol. LII, June, 1962, pp. 492–95.

KLEIN, L. R. "Comment on Solving the Wharton Model." *Review of Economics and Statistics,* Vol. XLIX, November, 1967.

KURIBAYASHI, S. "Variance of Forecasts for an Econometric Model." *The Economic Studies Quarterly,* Vol. XVII, September, 1967, p. 343.

LESER, C. E. V. "The Role of Macroeconomic Models in Short-Term Forecasting." *Econometrica,* Vol. XXXIV, October, 1966, p. 133.

MAY, F. B. "The Voice of Apollo: Historical Trends in Business Forecasting." *Social Science Quarterly,* Vol. L, June, 1969.

MINCER, J. *Economic Forecasts and Expectations: Analysis of Fore-*

casting Behavior and Performance. New York: National Bureau of Economic Research, 1969.

NERLOVE, M. "A Tabular Survey of Macro-Economic Models." *International Economic Review,* Vol. VII, 1966, pp. 127–75.

ROBINSON, C. "Some Principles of Forecasting in Business." *Journal of Industrial Economics,* Vol. XIV, November, 1965.

STEKLER, H. O. "An Evaluation of Quarterly Judgmental Economic Forecasts." *Journal of Business,* Vol. XLI, July, 1968.

——. "Forecasting with Econometric Models: An Evaluation." *Econometrica,* Vol. XXXVI, July/October, 1968, pp. 437–63.

——, and SUSAN W. BURCH. "Selected Economic Data: Accuracy vs. Reporting Speed," *Journal of the American Statistical Association,* Vol. XIII, June, 1968.

THEIL, H., and M. SCHOLES. "Forecast Evaluation Based on Multiplicative Decomposition of Mean Square Errors," *Econometrica,* Vol. XXXV, January, 1967, p. 125.

TULL, D. S. "The Relationship of Actual and Predicted Sales and Profits in New-Product Introductions." *Journal of Business,* Vol. XL, July, 1967.

Index

This book has been set in 12 point and 11 point Granjon, leaded 3 points. Chapter numbers and titles are in 18 point Helvetica. The size of the type page is 24 by 45 picas.